Know Your Playbook: Faith, Discipline, and Purpose in the Athletic Life

For wholesale inquiries, please reach out to greghendricks.life

Published by Radiant Publishing

Paperback ISBN: 978-1-963922-07-3

Cover Art By: Vince Freeman vfreeman08@yahoo.com

Introduction		i
How To Use This Book		iii
DAY 1	**Know Your Worth**	1
DAY 2	**Know Who You Worship**	7
DAY 3	**Know Your Word**	13
DAY 4	**Know Your Why**	19
DAY 5	**Understanding Your Identity in Christ**	25
DAY 6	**The Discipline of Daily Devotion**	31
DAY 7	**Worship in Every Moment**	37
DAY 8	**The Power of Scripture Memorization**	43
DAY 9	**Finding Strength in Weakness**	49
DAY 10	**Teamwork in Christ**	55
DAY 11	**Leadership Through Service**	61
DAY 12	**Integrity On and Off the Field**	67
DAY 13	**Perseverance Through Trials**	73
DAY 14	**Sharing Your Faith Story**	79
DAY 15	**The Importance of Rest**	85

DAY 16	**The Role of Humility**	91
DAY 17	**Cultivating Spiritual Discipline**	97
DAY 18	**Overcoming Temptation**	103
DAY 19	**The Power of a Positive Attitude**	109
DAY 20	**Faith as the Foundation of Team Unity**	115
DAY 21	**Facing Fear with Faith**	121
DAY 22	**Gratitude in Victory and Defeat**	127
DAY 23	**The Discipline of Forgiveness**	133
DAY 24	**The Witness of Work Ethic**	139
DAY 25	**The Role of Patience in Personal Growth**	145
DAY 26	**Endurance in Faith and Fitness**	151
DAY 27	**The Importance of Spiritual Mentors**	157
DAY 28	**Competing with Compassion**	163
DAY 29	**The Impact of a Christ-like Attitude**	169
DAY 30	**Unity in Diversity**	175
Conclusion		181

Introduction

In a world filled with noise, distractions, and endless challenges, finding one's path can seem daunting, stressful, and exhausting at times. For athletes in many sports, the playbook serves as a resource that outlines strategies, plays, and the principles needed to win competition either with a team, organization or individually. It also outlines the culture, mindset, and ethos of that organization or team. Similarly, in life and faith, a playbook is essential—serving as a guide that helps us navigate our spiritual journey of growth with purpose, clarity, and appropriate direction as we attempt to grow closer to God.

Hello, my name is Greg Hendricks. I have had the privilege of playing collegiate and professional sports. I have also been afforded the honor of coaching with professional and high school basketball teams. Currently, I serve as pastor and itinerant chaplin for professional sport teams and different organizations, helping to deepen their faith. I would like to introduce you to "Know Your Playbook." A resource designed to inspire, challenge, and equip you for your daily walk with Christ as an athlete. Drawing from my experiences as a collegiate and professional athlete, my current and ongoing service to Christ, and a pastor and mentor to many, my goal is to offer this playbook as a tool to help you discover your identity, purpose, and calling while developing your faith in Christ as a current or aspiring athlete.

As you delve into this playbook, remember that the journey with Christ is not a sprint but a marathon. It requires perseverance, dedication, surrender, and a heart willing to open up your lives before the Word of God. I invite you to explore the depths of your faith, to understand the playbook God has laid out for you (in the bible), and to live out your divine calling with passion, conviction, and purpose.

"Know Your Playbook" is more than just a resource; it's a compass for those seeking to deepen their relationship with God, to stand firm amidst trials, and to define your identity in Christ. We will embark on this journey together, equipped with the Word of God, guided by the Holy Spirit, and inspired by the goal of learning about our faith through the lens of Jesus.

My prayer for you, the athlete, is that this resource offers you additional strength and focus on your journey. That you would continue walking the path of faith and discipline in pursuit of excellence, both in and out of competition. This devotional book is crafted with the unique challenges and victories of the athletic journey in mind; this guide seeks to equip you, the athlete, with the wisdom, strength, and perseverance needed to navigate the competitive world of sports, the rigors of training, and the mental anguishes of competition while deepening your relationship with Christ.

Athletics is more than just a game or competition; it's a calling that requires dedication, sacrifice, and an unwavering commitment to excellence. As athletes, you are familiar with the rigorous demands of training, the thrill of competition, the agony of defeat, and the relentless pursuit of victory. However, beyond the physical discipline and tactical strategies lies a deeper, more profound battle—the battle for your heart, your character, and your soul.

In this journey, your greatest playbook is not one filled with strategies for physical dominance but rather one filled with spiritual strengthening, the living Word of God. It offers guidance, encouragement, and the keys to true victory. "Know Your Playbook" is designed to bridge the gap between your athletic endeavors and your spiritual growth, recognizing that true success is not merely measured by trophies, competition, the grind or accolades but by the depth of your relationship with Christ and the impact of your life on others, in and out of competition. Welcome to your playbook for navigating faith and athletics—let's lock in and grow!

—Greg Hendricks

How to use this book

"Know your playbook" is designed to give you a spiritual roadmap for your athletic journey. Within the 30-day devotional setting, you're going to find diverse content that covers the spiritual journey and the athletic journey. Each devotional is filled with inspiration, scripture, reflections, action steps and a prayer. As you dive into this amazing resource, take time and work through sections and keep them on your heart and your mind as you set out to accomplish great things in your athletic careers and personal journeys of faith.

GAINING INSPIRATION AND KNOWLEDGE

This playbook draws a compelling parallel between the discipline required for athletic training and spiritual growth. Just as athletes commit to rigorous physical training, spiritual disciplines—prayer, scripture reading, worship, and fellowship—are presented as essential practices for strengthening one's faith. This disciplined approach to spirituality and faith resonates with athletes accustomed to structured training regimens, encouraging them to apply the same dedication to their relationship with God.

SCRIPTURE

Perhaps the most striking theme is the call to live out one's purpose in Christ. "Know Your Playbook" doesn't just encourage athletes to excel in their sport but to use their platform for God's glory while competing as an athlete. It's a reminder that your influence extends beyond the game, offering opportunities to witness, serve, and lead others toward Christ. This holistic view of purpose—where athletic achievement and spiritual growth are intertwined— inspires athletes to pursue a legacy that lasts beyond their sporting careers.

REFLECTION AND ACTION: A CALL TO HOLISTIC GROWTH

Throughout the playbook, you will see the integration of reflection questions and actionable steps. This serves as a catalyst for holistic growth. Athletes are not only encouraged to reflect on their spiritual journey but are also provided with practical ways to live out their faith. This approach fosters a dynamic, active faith that influences every area of life, including athletic endeavors.

PRAYER

Every devotion concludes with a prayer to God. This is to establish a regular conversation between you and God. This is a fantastic way to pray through our lives, struggles, and dreams and to connect with God in your journey of growth consistently. Think of prayer as more of an active conversation with God than a religious routine, and you will start to see the results of your prayers and the development of your prayer life come alive.

THE ATHLETE'S HEART: DISCIPLINE AND DEVOTION

As an athlete, you understand the value of discipline, the importance of a focused mind, and the power of a devoted heart. You put these attributes into daily training to be able to perform at your optimum capacity for your team or the sport that you are competing in. These traits are not only essential for achieving athletic excellence but are also foundational to your spiritual journey of growth. Just as you train your body and hone your skills for competition, so too must you cultivate your heart, mind, and soul through prayer, study of scripture, and fellowship with other followers of Christ.

This guide will walk you through some essential aspects of living out your faith in the context of athletics, from understanding your identity in Christ to the significance of worship, understanding how to handle setbacks, the importance of knowing God's Word, and discovering your purpose. Each section is crafted to challenge, inspire, and equip you to live a life of faith that transcends the boundaries of sports, impacting your teammates, coaches, fans, and the broader community for Christ through your life and career.

NAVIGATING CHALLENGES WITH FAITH

An athlete's path is fraught with challenges—physical injuries, competitive pressures, temptations to compromise integrity for success, and the struggle to balance sport, academics, and personal life. These trials test not only your physical and mental resilience but also your faith. "Know Your Playbook" addresses these challenges head-on, offering biblical wisdom and practical advice for navigating them with grace and strength, grounded in your identity as a child of God.

BUILDING A LEGACY OF FAITH AND EXCELLENCE

Your journey as a Christian athlete is about more than just personal achievement; it's about building a legacy that reflects the character of Christ, inspires others to pursue excellence in all areas of life, and draws them to the love and truth of the gospel. This guide is your companion in that journey, encouraging you to live out your faith boldly and authentically, using your platform in athletics as a powerful tool for witnessing and ministry.

As you delve into "Know Your Playbook," may you be inspired to see your athletic career as a mission field ripe with opportunities to glorify God, serve others, and make an eternal impact as you aspire to compete. Remember, the ultimate victory is not found in the accolades of this world but in hearing the words, "Well done, good and faithful servant," from the one who has called you to this race, and has given you the ability and drive to compete in athletics.

Let us embark on this journey together with hearts open to God's leading, ready to grow, serve, and compete in a way that honors Him above all. Welcome to your playbook for navigating faith and athletics—let's go, let's grow, let's get it!!!

DAY ONE
Know Your Worth

“

*I find my strength
not in pretending to be strong,
but in being real with God
about my weaknesses.*

”

—TIM TEBOW

EMBRACING YOUR IDENTITY IN CHRIST: WHAT TEAM DO YOU PLAY FOR?

In the faith journey, understanding and embracing your identity in Christ is paramount. It is the bedrock upon which every other aspect of your spiritual life is built. In sports and amid competition and training, the target of who you represent is always at the forefront of your why. Whether it's the team you play for, the competitor you inspire to be, or the Championships you are trying to achieve. At most times, you are training and competing for something that is a culmination of months, sometimes years, of hard work and sacrifice not only from you, but people connected to you. The amount of effort put into achieving success constantly pushes you beyond your own idea of what you are physically and mentally able to do. It takes you to depths of yourself that you didn't even know were accessible until you decided to pursue it at all costs. In your walk in faith, this same depth of sacrifice should be a part of your hunger to deepen your identity in God. Understanding true identity starts with deep sacrifice. It requires vulnerability, surrender, and a desire to go deep with God. Our highest importance is recognizing our identity not as the world sees us but as God sees us—valued, chosen, and destined for a purpose far greater than any earthly achievement.

THE ENEMY'S STRATEGY AGAINST YOUR IDENTITY

Just as a well-prepared athlete knows the tactics of the opposing team, it's vital to recognize that the enemy, Satan, has a game plan designed to undermine your identity in Christ. He aims to sow seeds of doubt, confusion, and discouragement, hoping to distract you from your divine calling and purpose. The first step in countering this strategy is awareness. By understanding the tactics used against us, we can better arm ourselves with the truth of God's Word.

SCRIPTURE: YOUR PLAYBOOK FOR IDENTITY

The Bible is filled with passages that affirm our identity in Christ. These playbook truths are not just words on a page but life-giving truths meant to be believed, declared, and lived out. God has designed these plays from the beginning to equip you to not only know your opposition's tactics but also how to combat them to victory in your life. Take a look at what God says about you, along with additional verses, to reinforce your understanding of who you are in Christ.

- **Ephesians 2:10** - "For we are his workmanship, created in Christ Jesus for good works, which God prepared beforehand, that we should walk in them." This verse not only affirms your worth but also your purpose. As God's workmanship, you are crafted with precision, care, and intentionality. Each of you is created for specific good works that God has prepared in advance for you to do. Reflect on this truth: you are not an accident or an afterthought; you are a divine creation with a purpose ordained by God Himself. Your playbook, written by God, says that you are designed by Him, with good works to do for Him. Your opposition will try to get you to abandon this as you progress through life, especially during the tough times or in seasons of transition.

- **2 Corinthians 5:17** - "Therefore, if anyone is in Christ, he is a new creation. The old has passed away; behold, the new has come." In Christ, we are given a fresh start, a new identity. The past, with all its failures, mistakes, and sins, is gone. The seasons where we fall or come up short should not define what we're not; they should define who we really are in Christ. Adversity or tumultuous seasons should reveal what kingdom has dominion inside of us. The Kingdom of God, or the kingdom of man. This verse is a powerful reminder of the transformative power of salvation and our new life in Christ. It challenges us to live in the reality of our new identity, shedding the old self and embracing the new creation we have become.

- **Colossians 3:3** - "For you have died, and your life is hidden with Christ in God." This passage speaks to the security of our identity in Christ. Hidden with Christ in God implies protection, a safekeeping of our true selves in the divine. It's a profound truth that our life, our identity, is now intertwined with Christ's. Regardless of our challenges or trials, our identity remains secure and unshakeable in Him. Times of despair or even great success will often reveal if we are true to this core principle in our DNA as image-bearers of God.

REFLECTING ON YOUR IDENTITY

As you meditate on these scriptures, consider their implications for your daily life. As an athlete, everyday training brings you a step closer to achieving success in your sport or craft. Your ability to understand your identity is a core value for strengthening your faith.

- How does knowing you are God's workmanship change the way you view yourself and your purpose?

- What does it mean for you to live as a new creation, especially in areas where you struggle to let go of the past?

- How can the truth that your life is hidden with Christ in God provide peace and security, even amid uncertainty?

ACTION POINTS

- **Daily Declarations:** Create a list of personal affirmations based on the scriptures mentioned. Declare these truths over your life each morning. For example, "I am God's workmanship, created in Christ Jesus for good works."

- **Identity Journal**: Start an identity journal where you document your journey of discovering your identity in Christ. Include scripture meditations, prayers, and any revelations or encouragements God provides.

- **Community Engagement**: Share your journey of understanding your identity in Christ with a trusted friend or mentor. Engage in discussions about identity in small groups, on your team, with your chaplin or Bible studies to encourage and learn from one another.

Prayer for Identity

Heavenly Father, I thank You for creating me
in Your image, crafting me with purpose,
and offering me a new life in Christ.
Help me to see myself as You see me—
valued, chosen, and loved.
Strengthen my understanding of my
identity in You, and empower me to live out
the good works You have prepared for me.
Protect me from the enemy's lies, and anchor
my identity securely in Your truth.
In Jesus' name, Amen.

DAY TWO

Know Who You Worship

"

Talent is God-given. Be humble.
Fame is man-given. Be grateful.
Conceit is self-given. Be careful.

"

—JOHN WOODEN

In the life of an athlete, discipline, focus, and dedication are not just traits but necessities for success. These same qualities are essential in our spiritual lives, particularly in worship. Worship is not merely an act of singing or attending church services; it's a lifestyle, a continuous surrender of every moment, every victory, and every struggle to God. It's an overflow of daily life of surrender and dedication to God's purpose in all areas of our life. This section explores the transformative power of worship in the life of a believer, especially for athletes who are constantly under the spotlight and pressure of performance.

WORSHIP AS A WEAPON OF WARFARE

In the competitive world of sports, athletes are often taught to use their skills, strategies, and mental toughness as abilities against their opponents. Similarly, in our spiritual lives, worship serves as our weapon of warfare against the enemy's attacks. But this battle is not against flesh and blood; it's against spiritual forces of evil (Ephesians 6:12). When we worship, we're not just singing songs; we're declaring our allegiance to God, aligning our hearts with His and standing firm against the enemy's schemes. You are practicing daily, not the ability to sing songs, but to develop a core practice and value of how to surrender before God. This can come through the expression of prayer, singing, repentance, or rejoicing. You are developing the habit of dialoguing daily about all things with your maker.

THE CHALLENGE OF KEEPING WORSHIP-CENTERED

Worship can take many forms beyond singing or praying. It's in the dedication to training, the respect for one's body as a temple of the Holy Spirit, the humility in victory, and the grace in defeat. Worship is recognizing that every game, every practice, and every moment of your career is an opportunity to glorify God, and it is a gift to you to be able to do so.

For an athlete, the roar of the crowd, the accolades, and the spotlight can easily become intoxicating, subtly shifting the focus from worshiping God to basking in the glory of one's achievements or even being worshiped yourself (self-idolization). The enemy seeks to steal our worship by tempting us to idolize our success, talents, or even the game itself. In this battle for our worship, it's crucial to remember that every talent, every opportunity, and every victory comes from God. Remember, "Anything that consumes your attention also competes for your affection."

SCRIPTURE: THE PLAYBOOK OF WORSHIP

To navigate the challenges of worship in a world filled with distractions, we turn to the playbook of scriptures that guide us back to the heart of worship. Read these scriptures and pray them out loud in order to see their true benefit.

- **John 4:24** - "God is spirit, and those who worship him must worship in spirit and truth." This verse reminds us that true worship transcends physical location or external rituals; it's about the posture of our hearts towards God, worshiping Him with authenticity and a deep sense of reverence, even amid victory or defeat.

- **Isaiah 12:5** - "Sing praises to the Lord, for he has done gloriously; let this be made known in all the earth." Here, the call to worship is also a call to testify to God's goodness and glory, sharing with the world the source of our strength, talent, and success, not just on the stage of competition but in the privacy of our conversations with friends or in our moments when we dream of achieving that championship. Worship in God helps us stay postured with the right motive to achieve the success we desire to see.

REFLECTION QUESTIONS

It's time to consider the reality of worship in your life. What environment encourages you to have a heart filled with worship to God and what takes away from that? contemplate how worship advances you in your purpose and in your calling.

- Can you recall a time when your achievements or the game itself began to consume more of your attention and affection than your worship of God?
- How did you realize this, and what steps did you take to refocus your worship on God?
- How do you incorporate worship into your routine as an athlete?
- Are there practices or disciplines you've found helpful in keeping God at the center of your athletic career?

ACTION POINTS

- **Worship Before Competing**: Before each game, practice, or training session, take a moment to dedicate your efforts to God. This can be a short prayer, a scripture reading, or a moment of silence to focus your mind and heart on God.

- **Create a Worship Playlist**: Compile a playlist of worship songs that inspire and uplift you. Listen to this playlist during workouts, before games, or in your downtime to keep your spirit attuned to God's presence. And your affection is targeted in the right direction.
- **Weekly Worship Reflection**: Set aside time each week to reflect on where you've seen God's hand in your life and athletic career. Journal these reflections as a testament to God's faithfulness and as a reminder of why you worship.

Prayer for Worship

Lord, I thank You for the talents and opportunities You've given me in my athletic career. Help me always remember that my ultimate purpose is to glorify You in victory and defeat. Teach me to worship You in spirit and truth, keeping You at the center of everything I do. May my life be a continuous act of worship, reflecting Your love and grace to those around me.
In Jesus' name, Amen.

DAY THREE
Know Your Word

"

The will to win is important,
but the will to prepare is vital.

"

—JOE PATERNO

Knowledge of the game is crucial in competitive athletics. An athlete studies the playbook meticulously, watches film, with the goal to understand strategies, plays , and the opponent's tendencies. This discipline and dedication to knowledge are paralleled in our spiritual journey through studying and applying God's Word. In this section, we will look at the transformative power of the Bible in a believer's life, especially for athletes. An athlete's discipline in sport can serve as a strength to fuel their approach to spiritual growth.

THE BIBLE: YOUR ULTIMATE PLAYBOOK

Just as a detailed playbook guides an athlete to victory, the Bible is our ultimate playbook for life. It contains the strategies we need to navigate life's challenges, the encouragement to keep us going when we face setbacks, and the wisdom to make the right decisions both in and out of competition. Understanding God's Word is not just about reading; it's about allowing it to penetrate our hearts and transform our lives. We gain the ability to help shape our families and define our thought patterns through our journey in life.

THE REVELATION OF GOD'S WORD IN RELATION TO GOD'S HEART

The relationship between an athlete and their coach is built on trust, communication, and understanding. The coach's playbook is effective not just because of the plays it contains but because it is an extension of the coach's philosophy, heart, and strategy for winning. Similarly, the Bible is God's revelation to us, a direct communication from our Creator, Coach, and Father. It reveals His heart, desires for us, and ultimate plan for redemption for humanity in the life of Jesus. When we study the Bible, we're not just learning rules or stories; we're deepening our relationship with God, understanding His heart, and aligning our lives with His purposes and His character.

THE CHALLENGE OF REMAINING IN TRUTH

Athletes understand the importance of consistency and discipline in training to achieve peak performance. This principle applies to our spiritual life as well. Many face challenges not in the initial encounter with God's Word but in consistently engaging with scripture and applying it to their lives. The enemy seeks to distort, distract, and discourage us from the truth of God's Word. Let me say this to you: Partial truth, as, is a full lie! It's crucial to arm yourselves with the full truth of scripture, allowing it to guide you in every aspect of your lives.

SCRIPTURE: DEEPENING YOUR PLAYBOOK KNOWLEDGE

Training your heart and mind with the Word of God is vital for your growth. The Bible has not only stood the test of time but has also been instrumental in the growth of billions around the globe. Its truth is not just about principles to live by but also about an invitation to get to know God. We must not ignore the vital truth that's available within the Word of God. The invitation for you is to become a student of the Word.

- **John 8:32** - "And you will know the truth, and the truth will set you free." This verse underscores the liberating power of truth. For an athlete, freedom is found in the mastery of their sport through the process of the work. Similarly, spiritual freedom and victory are found in the time put in to read the Word, learn His truths, and apply those truths in our lives.

- **Psalm 119:105** - "Your word is a lamp to my feet and a light to my path." Just as a coach's advice can illuminate the next step for an athlete or help the athlete compete at the highest level of competition, God's Word illuminates our path, guiding us through life's challenges and decisions.

- **Hebrews 4:12** - "For the Word of God is alive and active. Sharper than any double-edged sword, it penetrates even to divide soul and spirit, joints and marrow; it judges the thoughts and attitudes of the heart." In sports, feedback and analysis are vital for improvement. We need feedback to help the athlete succeed in the competition. The Word of God acts as the ultimate feedback mechanism, revealing our innermost thoughts and guiding our growth.

REFLECTION QUESTIONS

Reflecting on the Word of God will surround you with your purpose and higher calling. It will compel you to change and become a better version of yourself. As you consider the Word of God for yourself today, make it a habit to return to it in times of victory and in times of defeat.

- How has your engagement with God's Word impacted your athletic and personal life?

- What practical steps can you take to deepen your understanding of the Bible and integrate its truths into your daily routines?

- Reflect on Biblical characters and ask yourself how you relate to them.

ACTION POINTS INTEGRATING THE WORD INTO YOUR ATHLETIC LIFE

- **Daily Study**: Just as daily practice is essential for athletic improvement, daily Bible study is crucial for spiritual growth. Dedicate a specific time daily to read, study, and meditate on God's Word. Start with a minimum of 10 min with the target of building up to 1 hour daily.

- **Scripture Memorization**: Athletes memorize plays until they become second nature. Similarly, memorize scripture to fortify your heart and mind against enemy attacks and guide your decisions. Start with the ones that define who you are in God. And read one proverb a day.

- **Application Through Reflection**: After each game or practice, athletes review their performance to identify areas for improvement. They watch films with a coach or by themselves to see areas of improvement. Apply this principle to your spiritual life by reflecting on how you can apply the day's scripture in your personal and athletic life. Recall your day and see if something you are memorizing applies to your growth in your faith. If there is not, start by applying your daily declaration to yourself.

Prayer for Understanding of the Word

Heavenly Father, I thank You for Your Word,
a lamp unto my feet and a light unto my path.
Grant me the discipline, understanding, and
wisdom to study Your Word diligently.
Help me apply it to my life as an athlete and
a follower. May Your truths penetrate
my heart, guiding my decisions,
strengthening my resolve, and deepening
my relationship with You. Help me stand firm
in Your Word, equipped to face life's challenges
and temptations with courage and integrity.
Let Your Word be alive and active in me,
transforming me from the inside out and enabling
me to reflect Your love and grace in all I do.
In Jesus' name, Amen.

DAY FOUR
Know Your Why

“

I think goals should never be easy; they should force you to work, even if they are uncomfortable at the time.

”

—MICHAEL PHELPS

For athletes, the drive to excel, push beyond limits, and overcome adversity is fueled by a powerful "why"—a reason beyond medals, accolades, or records. This internal motivation propels them through the rigors of training and competition, shaping their identity and approach to life. Similarly, in our faith journey, understanding our "why" in Christ—our purpose as believers—provides the foundation and motivation for everything we do, both in and out of the sports arena.

THE INTERSECTION OF FAITH AND ATHLETICISM

Athletes are often admired for their physical strength, mental toughness, and relentless pursuit of excellence. When rooted in a Christ-centered purpose, these qualities can serve as a powerful testimony of faith, perseverance, and reliance on God's strength. For the believer-athlete, the pursuit of excellence in sport becomes an act of worship, a means to glorify God, and a platform to share the gospel as you train and compete.

UNDERSTANDING YOUR PURPOSE IN CHRIST

Your purpose in Christ transcends your athletic achievements. It's about embodying the values of the Kingdom of God—love, service, humility, and integrity, to name a few—in every aspect of your life, including your sport. It's about recognizing that every talent, opportunity, and platform is given by God and for God. This understanding shifts the focus from personal glory to God's glory and from self-fulfillment to fulfilling God's mission through all the abilities and ambition afforded to you.

Athletes face unique pressures—from the temptation to compromise values for success to the idolization of achievement to the challenge of balancing sport and faith. Overcoming these challenges requires a steadfast commitment to your purpose in Christ and reliance on His strength and guidance even amidst of competition. You can strengthen this by spending time in His Word, praying, and talking about Him and who He is in your life and the lives of others.

SCRIPTURE: THE FOUNDATION OF OUR PURPOSE

The best way to find our identity in God is to serve the scriptures and find out what they say. If you ever have a question about the scripture, always refer back to the life of Jesus because he is the cornerstone of your faith.

- **Matthew 28:18-19** - "And Jesus came and spoke to them, saying, 'All authority has been given to Me in heaven and on earth. Go therefore and make disciples of all the nations, baptizing them in the name of the Father and of the Son and of the Holy Spirit.'" This Great Commission highlights the ultimate purpose of every believer: to make disciples. For athlete-believers, this means using your influence and platform to share Christ's love and message with others, whether teammates, fans, or the global community.

- **1 Corinthians 9:24-27** - Paul uses athletic imagery to describe the Christian life, emphasizing discipline, self-control, and the goal of winning an imperishable crown. This passage can inspire athletes to see their physical discipline as a metaphor for spiritual discipline, aiming not just for earthly victories but for eternal rewards.

- **1 John 3:2** "Dear friends, now we are children of God, and what we will be has not yet been made known. But we know that when Christ appears, we shall be like him, for we shall see him as he is." The revelation and knowledge of who you are is secondary to the knowledge of whos you are. You are a child of God, and no one can take that away from you.

REFLECTION QUESTIONS

Reflecting on your purpose is integral to refining it. Consistently examining your life as a third party is very helpful. Separate yourself from your thoughts and reflect on your values as if you're looking into a window of your life. This will help you not come up with artificial identities but rather pick and choose the values that are truly great for you in order for you to succeed both in faith and as an athlete.

- How does your identity in Christ influence your identity as an athlete?

- What challenges have you faced in integrating your faith with your sport, and how have you addressed them?

- In what ways can you use your athletic platform to further God's Kingdom?

ACTION POINTS: LIVING OUT YOUR PURPOSE

- **Integrate Faith and Sport**: One way to do this is to view your sport as a ministry at any level of competition. As you compete at any level of sport, every opportunity, whether it be practice, treatment, games, or team get-togethers, your performance, work ethic, and interactions with others reflect Christ's love and excellence in your life. The way you carry yourself and how you respond in your environments offer greater opportunities to talk about who drives you.

- **Service**: Look for opportunities to serve within your team, community, and beyond. This could mean mentoring younger athletes, volunteering for charitable causes, or simply being a supportive teammate. Also, be a leader who gathers others together for a time of fellowship and connection.

- **Witnessing**: Use your platform to share your faith story. This could be through interviews, social media, speaking engagements, or personal conversations. Remember, your story can be a powerful tool in God's hands. You don't have to be forceful, but be authentic. Remember, people are more attracted to the authenticity of your relationship with God.

Prayer for Living Out Your Purpose:

Lord, I thank You for the talents
You've bestowed upon me and the
platform of athletics You've provided.
Help me to understand and embrace
my purpose in You, using every moment
in and out of competition to glorify Your name.
Give me the strength to face challenges
with grace, the wisdom to navigate
the pressures of competition,
and the courage to share Your love
with others. May my life reflect Your light,
drawing others to know You.
In Jesus' Name, Amen.

DAY FIVE

Understanding Your Identity in Christ

"

I am a Christian that loves the Lord that just happens to play football.

"

—SHAUN ALEXANDER

Who you are and what you do are very different realities in life. We often mix up the two as we desire to accomplish great things. We think that we are a composite of our accomplishments or our failures. Nothing could be further from the truth. Our identity goes far beyond seasonal recognition; it's rooted in something eternal. We have an identity in Christ first and foremost in our lives. We can go our entire lives without knowing that. The first stage of understanding your identity is acknowledging where you came from and who you belong to.

KNOWING WHO YOU ARE

You were brought into this world by divine design, and God knows every hair on your head. If you're bald, he knows how many hairs you had when you were born. Why does this matter? The intimate details of our lives are well known to God because we were made in His image. As we get to know Jesus, we get to know ourselves because we were made to look like him in our love and acceptance of everyone. We were made to be like him in our accomplishments and exploits.

MOLD ME INTO SOMETHING GREAT

We can be shaped and molded by anything and everything in this world. Wouldn't you prefer to be transformed into your creator's image rather than a corruptible image of something around you? The difference is truly life-changing. As you think within yourself, consider who made you in the investment that they made in you. You're special, and God knows that. That's why he put you here. You have great things in you because you came from greatness. You are not a composite of your accomplishments or your failures. You are His!

SCRIPTURE IS OUR IDENTITY IN GOD

You were made in the image of God, and the more you get to know Christ Jesus, the more you will get to know yourself. Every scripture is an invitation to get to know an aspect of God's character that you can directly apply to your own life.

- **Ephesians 2:10** - "For we are his workmanship, created in Christ Jesus for good works, which God prepared beforehand, that we should walk in them." We were made by God and given a roadmap for how we should walk through life. The roadmap for good works is visible in the life of Christ. No one should question what they should do because the path is clear.

- **1 Peter 2:9:** "But you are a chosen generation, a royal priesthood, a holy nation, His own special people, that you may proclaim the praises of Him who called you out of darkness into His marvelous light." Your association with God makes you a special person. If you feel like you're taking a different path, that's because you are. You are set apart for a purpose. Many are called, but few answer.

- **1 Samuel 12:22:** "For the Lord will not forsake His people, for His great name's sake, because it has pleased the Lord to make you His people." Once you're in Christ, how could you forsake Himself? Those who are in him operate from a positional authority that comes from God. If you're with him, then who could be against him? No one?

REFLECTIONS

Just as an athlete finds identity in their sport, your true identity is rooted in Christ. You are God's masterpiece, created with purpose and intentionality. Don't focus on the flaws that you see in the sin that you may have. Focus on who you should become. As your gaze increases on God, your flaws will be covered by him, along with your sins.

- What makes you different than everyone else?

- Consider the odds of you being born; it's nearly impossible to count.

- How would you live your life differently if you knew that you were made in the image of God?

ACTION POINTS

- **Application:** Reflect on your unique gifts and how they can be used for God's glory in your sport and daily life. What separates you from everyone else? What did God give you that he didn't give the person next to you?

- **Identity Journal:** Write down a few verses that speak to you about your identity in God and hang them on your wall or in your locker so you are reminded of your true identity daily.

- **Community Engagement**: Talk openly about what makes you unique in this world and discuss the characteristics and attributes that you see in yourself and in those around you according to how God sees you and them. The more you identify with God, the more you will experience that reality.

Prayer for Understanding Our Identity in Christ

Father, thank you for revealing yourself to me
through your Son Jesus. I'm so thankful
that you made me in His image.
Help me understand the investments
you've made in me so I can recognize you
in all I see. Thank you, God,
for helping me with the perspective
you want me to have about myself and
those around me. Open my eyes to see
when I am not operating in the identity
that you gave me and lead me down
a path of righteousness.
In Jesus name, amen.

DAY SIX

The Discipline of Daily Devotion

"

Sportsmanship for me is when a guy walks off the court, and you really can't tell whether he won or lost when he carries himself with pride either way.

"

—JIM COURIER

PRACTICE AND REPETITION CULTIVATE OUR HEARTS

Every morning, as you wake up and plan how to execute the day, whether it's workouts, practice, or competition, you have instilled devotion and discipline in yourself. You know it's necessary to show up and participate and give your best regardless of how you feel, what's on your mind, or what might be in your way. This discipline and daily devotion are essential for you to become the best. This is one of the first things you learn when advancing in any sport.

DAILY DEVOTION IS A SPIRITUAL JOURNEY

Now, let's consider disciplining daily devotion in your spiritual journey. You're not anchored in life unless you have discipline and devotion to God. You will get tossed around by every whim, strong wind or trial and tribulation that comes in your direction if you're not anchored in God. You can see the fruit of your daily devotion to your sport because you're putting in the work and seeing the results. The same is evident in your faith journey. If you put in the work, you'll start to see the results. This goes far beyond the understanding of salvation because it's transformative for the here and now.

OUR HEARTS DETERMINE OUR DEVOTION

Devotion is an attitude in the heart. You could practice something and not care for it. This isn't how our walk with God is birthed. Our hearts and our minds need to be fully involved because it's our invisible attributes that God cares most about. Time is undoubtedly a considerable factor in our devotion because it's the only thing we can't get more of. So, how valuable is it to someone and to God, that you give your time to them? Your time is extremely valuable. When you show up and participate in an active relationship with God through daily devotion, he will show up for you because he can trust you, and you both are familiar with each other.

When we wake up, we should give God our first fruits (the first part of our day and thoughts), perhaps even before everyone else is awake. We should turn our hearts to him for the sake of our relationship and spend time with him. Consider his words, lessons, and dreams as your first thoughts of the day. This will establish consistency within you and make you desire him first in your life. Once your heart is set on him, then you will know who to go to when things get tough, and you won't question your relationship with him because you'll be anchored in him, and he'll be your source of life, joy, and success. Even when competition, life, or your journey is being challenged.

SCRIPTURES ON DEVOTION

There's nothing new under the sun. You simply apply yourself to the Word of God it will reveal itself to you. Your devotion is truly up to you and the Word of God is ready for you to embrace it. As you begin to apply yourself through devotion you will realize its fruits and its rewards.

- **Scripture:** Joshua 1:8 - "Keep this Book of the Law always on your lips; meditate on it day and night, so that you may be careful to do everything written in it. Then you will be prosperous and successful."

Keeping the Word of God active within our lives is essential so that we do not be led astray.

- **Hebrews 12:11** - "For the moment all discipline seems painful rather than pleasant, but later it yields the peaceful fruit of righteousness to those who have been trained by it." This scripture highlights the importance of process and not trying to skip out on the refinement of life. We receive a greater reward when we push through and develop discipline.

- **Proverbs 12:1** - "Whoever loves discipline loves knowledge, but he who hates reproof is stupid." Our access to the greater things in life sometimes comes through reproof. We should embrace life-transforming challenges because they'll make us better people. If we avoid refinement, then are we cementing our inability to move forward and grow?

REFLECTIONS

Discipline in training is mirrored in spiritual growth in the same area. Consistent engagement with God's Word equips you for every challenge. Consider spiritual discipline that applies your heart, mind, and body to a process that you attribute to God. Develop within yourself the ability to be steady, consistent, and faithful. You will love yourself more, and so will the people around you.

- How can you restructure your lives to be more devoted to God?

- What's one thing that you believe that God wants from you every day?

- Think back to the last time you felt the closest to God; what were you doing?

ACTION POINTS

- **Application:** Commit to a specific time each day for Bible study and prayer. Apply yourself. Consider this time extremely important and put it on the top of your calendar.

- **Identity Journal**: Cement your thoughts and process by writing down an aspect of your devotion. This will help you track your progress and connection with God and go back to see where he has come through for you.

- **Daily Declarations**: Declaring scripture over your life is an incredible exercise that reminds you of who he is and who you are in him. Consider using scriptural declarations as part of your devotion.

Prayer for Discipline and Devotion

Lord, I thank you for showing me what
it's like to be devoted. You are more devoted to me
than I could ever imagine. Thank you for allowing
me to be a recipient of your devotion. I pray that I
can understand your heart and your perspective
within your devotion so that I can have my own.
Show me the characteristics and attributes
of those with pure, steadfast devotion to God
so that I may assimilate their heart towards you.
Thank you for your graciousness and your love.
In Jesus name, amen.

DAY SEVEN

Worship in Every Moment

"

Excellence is not a singular act but a habit.
You are what you do repeatedly.

"

—SHAQUILLE O'NEAL

Most consider times of worship to be on Sunday when you are listening to the band play your favorite song, and you sing along. However, our lives are an act of worship unto God. When we fill our hearts with thankfulness for the things that we have, that's a form of worship. When we demonstrate excellence in our sport or performance or our training, that is also an act of worship. As a matter of fact, it's possible to worship within everything that we do.

WORSHIP IS A LIFESTYLE

Not only is worship a lifestyle, but it's also a mindset and an attitude of our heart. This is why the considerations of our heart and our mind are so vital to our internal well-being. If an attitude of worship is first and foremost in our lives, then we will quickly dissuade the things that take away from that, like bitterness, hatred, and divisiveness. Instead, we will consider the people around us, our teammates, and our peers as a part of this incredible environment that has been cultivated by worship within us unto God.

Obstacles will always be in front of us; that's the nature of life. If you remove one obstacle, you'll have another; that's just how it works. We worship God not because it feels good but because sometimes it doesn't. We worship God because we were born too. If we don't worship Him, then we worship other things that could destroy us. There's a small minority of people who don't worship anything, but in fact, they worship their ideals, they worship others, or they worship their logic. We all worship every day, whether you know it or not. However, the question is, who are you worshiping? Whoever you worship, you will become like. That is why we need to set our hearts to worship God and God alone.

OUR PRIORITIES

What's possible when we participate in a lifestyle of worship? Only time can tell, but it's evident in the lives that have gone before us. Even when things weren't going according to plan for David, who is the soon-coming King, he continually made himself available to worship. This is a lesson for us that worship is a lifestyle and is not just a convenience when everything is going according to plan. We worship God in our thoughts and in our hearts. Those who truly want everything out of life prioritize God in everything that they do. Worship is a part of that process.

SCRIPTURE: WORSHIP ALWAYS

When studying scripture, you'll quickly see God's emphasis on worship, which is very important. The children of God in Israel didn't always get it right. They often worshiped the wrong things, and it brought about destruction upon themselves. Let's pray to advertise God in our worship, and we will see the fruit of it in our lives. You will also see the benefits in your careers as competitive athletes.

- **Romans 12:1** "Therefore, I urge you, brothers and sisters, in view of God's mercy, to offer your bodies as a living sacrifice, holy and pleasing to God—this is your true and proper worship." Worship is not just singing a song; It's a lifestyle. Everything we do is an act of worship to God, according to Romans 12.

- **Jeremiah 20:13:** "Sing to the LORD! Give praise to the LORD! He rescues the life of the needy from the hands of the wicked." We also have the opportunity to worship within our troubles. This changes our attitude towards the situation and opens up the opportunity for God to show up and rescue us.

- **Psalms 75:1:** "We praise you, God, we praise you, for your name is near; people tell of your wonderful deeds." In this verse, God's name is his character or his nature. As his name is drawn near, we actually have access to his nature.

REFLECTIONS

Worship isn't confined to song or church services; it's living your life in a way that honors God, including in and out of competition. Living a life of worship takes a great bit of consideration and engagement. The way you talk to people, the way you think, and the way you act all testify to who he is in you and through you. Always remember your behavior will follow your belief.

- Consider ways within your heart that you can worship God in the middle of practice.

- Identify one way that worship has changed you and prioritize it.

- Consider the music that you listen to and make sure that it edifies you and lifts up God.

ACTION POINTS

Application: Identify one way to incorporate worship into your athletic routine today.

Daily Worship: Set aside 10 minutes each day to worship God. It doesn't have to be elaborate. Simply show up and thank him for who he is.

Community Engagement: Don't be afraid to incorporate thoughtful praise and consideration before others. Thank God in front of them and mean it. It will change your heart, your heart, and the atmosphere around you.

Prayer for Worship

Lord, I thank you for designing us to worship.
What a beautiful opportunity we are given.
In this life, we can give our time, resources,
and affection to anyone and everyone.
Help us to prioritize you in all that we do.
Help me to testify of your goodness
in everything that I do.
You alone are worthy of my praise.
Thank you, God, for allowing me to draw
near to you so that I can be more like you,
and less like the world.
I bless you, God, and thank you for
transforming me through daily worship.
In Jesus' name, amen.

DAY EIGHT

The Power of Scripture Memorization

“

Persistence can change failure into extraordinary achievement.

”

—MATT BIONDI

The blueprint for your life is found within the Word of God. As you consider powerful stories and memorable verses, they will continue to evolve within you because the Word of God is alive and active. Of course, you may find inspiration in certain verses because they can tell you to be a great person of high value and importance, but even beyond that, as you consider the Word of God and it grows in you, you're actually changed and its image.

There's tremendous importance in memorizing and remembering what God has said and done. First and foremost, as we keep his words in our hearts and minds, they lead us. The Word of God illuminates our path so that we walk in a straight line. Also, because we're focused on the Word of God, we are not distracted by the things that could destroy us. Instead, we are reassured in our walk and persevere when obstacles come before us.

THE WORD IS OUR PATH

God will be your guide in life, your thoughts, and your relationships If you let him. Men and women in the New and Old Testament who prioritized the Word of God and their hearts and Minds were able to overcome and accomplish great and marvelous things. The Word of God within itself has tremendous principles by which to live. We should grab hold of and see them come to pass because there's a tremendous reward within the Word. Furthermore, the

Word of God gives us access to a relationship with God; not only do we find out about him, but we are invited to get to know him. This is why it's so important for us to prioritize spending time with God, reading our Bibles, and praying.

ONE VERSE AT A TIME

Reading and memorizing the Word of God may seem like a big task. It is a big task that can be broken up into a lifetime of learning. Instead of getting overwhelmed by the idea of reading and trying to memorize your Bible, start with one verse. Read it out loud, say it out loud, think about it and pray about it. I imagine the next time that you consider that verse, it'll be much easier for you to recall it because it's now a part of you, and there's an aspect of God that's been revealed to you because of that verse. This is how you read and experience the Bible.

SCRIPTURES ON MEMORIZATION

Take time and consider the Word of God before you. It is an everlasting invitation to get to know God and yourself. Develop a level of importance and understanding around the Word of God; see you hold it in high esteem and value in your mind. Consider reading a verse three times. First, read a verse the way the original listeners would have read it. Second, read the verse again to look for context and meaning. Lastly, read it as though a teacher would as they prepare for their students.

- **Psalm 119:11** says, "I have hidden your word in my heart that I might not sin against you." Many struggle with sin because the Word of God is not in their hearts. If you're looking for the key to your breakthrough, it's within the Word of God.
- **Matthew 4:4** - But he answered, "It is written, 'Man shall not live by bread alone, but by every word that comes from the mouth of God.'" Jesus is

referencing the manna that came from heaven in the Old Testament. No longer do we look to our old institutional systems to provide us with salvation; we look to the Word of God.

- **Psalm 119:105** - "Your word is a lamp to my feet and a light to my path." If our heart is made pure, then our path will be easy. The Word of God illuminates whichever direction we walk because the considerations of our hearts are now guided.

REFLECTIONS

Just as athletes memorize plays, memorizing scripture equips you to face life's challenges with God's wisdom. It is a cognitive exercise that trains your heart's attitude and posture.

- Consider Psalms 119:105 on how it applies to your own life, and what it could mean to you.

- Start a Bible memorization plan. There are many available that take you through the Bible in one year.

- Ask yourself what is a verse that you should live by and search it out until you have an answer.

ACTION POINTS

- **Application:** Memorize a verse that speaks to your current situation or challenge.

- **Read, Read, Read:** Take three verses today, read them out loud, pray them out loud, read them fast, and read them slowly, and ask yourself what's different in your understanding.

- **Community Engagement**: Start a dialogue about verses that change your life with your friends and your family. Consider posting a verse on social media or hanging it in your locker or on your wall that inspires you every day.

Prayer for Scripture Memorization

Lord, thank you for providing us with
the Word of God as an Illuminating light
to our lives. I ask that you give me extra grace
in considering your words before my heart
and my mind. Help me to establish a routine
in which I prioritize you and your Word.
Thank you, God, for being so faithful and
everlasting in my life and never giving up on me.
Your Word is truly remarkable and life-changing,
and I want more of it in my life.
Thank you so much, God.
In Jesus name, amen.

DAY NINE

Finding Strength in Weakness

> "
>
> *There are only two options regarding commitment. You're either IN, or you're OUT. There is no such thing as life in-between.*
>
> "
>
> —PAT RILEY

HE IS STRONG WHEN WE ARE WEAK.

In moments of weakness, we have to rely on other parts of ourselves to compensate temporarily. This is an intriguing and Illuminating process that we go through to find hidden strengths within us. We may find ourselves with a physical injury at certain points during our journey. As we go about our healing, we will have to rely on other parts of ourselves to push through. If we break a finger, we tape it to the next one. If we hurt our ankle, we pivot on the other foot. The versatility of our adaption will bring us to another level in our sport.

Many of us might consider for the first time that we can persevere regardless of trials. One of the most amazing things visible in every sport is when our physical body is limited in some way, and we have to rely on our minds to overcome it. Perhaps our bodies are tired or in pain, but we can find a mental strength that allows us to push through and overcome the obstacles in front of us. No one can take our mental fortitude away. No one can stop our inner strength when our bodies are weak.

MINDSETS MAKE PEOPLE

The stories are endless about how athletes push through unbelievable odds to achieve great things. Even more than perseverance, we have the opportunity to find additional paths to success within ourselves. If we convince ourselves that we can achieve everything that we've set our hearts to regardless of how our body feels, what's stopping us now? This mindset of finding strength amid our weakness is available to you even now.

On a spiritual note, God is strong in the areas where we are weak and lacking and frail. Where we have fissures and fractures and limitations, he does not. We can rely on him to be there for us when we are weak. He doesn't expect us to be perfect and knows what we need. We can rely on him and lean on him just as John the Beloved did in the Bible. He laid his head upon Jesus's chest and listened to his heart. We can rely on God in the very same way. He will always be there for us.

SCRIPTURE ON FINDING STRENGTH IN WEAKNESS

Embracing God to fill a void in our lives starts in an area of realization. We have to be open and accepting of what God has to offer. We need to admit that we don't have it all together and that we are in need of help. This posture allows us to grow and accept what God has to offer for us. The soil of our heart will finally be ready for planting. Consider the Word of God as a seed planted in your heart.

- **2 Corinthians 12:9-10** - "But he said to me, 'My grace is sufficient for you, for my power is made perfect in weakness.' Therefore, I will boast all the more gladly about my weaknesses so that Christ's power may rest on me." Grace is the equivalent of life. The more grace we have, the more life we have. We receive empowered grace when we recognize how strong he is in our lives.

- **Ephesians 6:10–11:** "Finally, be strong in the Lord and in his mighty power. Put on the full armor of God so that you can take your stand against the devil's schemes." The armor of God is a physical representation of the infrastructure that will defend against the enemy in your heart and in your mind. We should take away from this verse that we are to actively put on the Word of God to receive its strength.

- **Philippians 4:11–13:** "I am not saying this because I am in need, for I have learned to be content whatever the circumstances. I know what it is to be in need and what it is to have plenty. I have learned the secret of being content in any and every situation, whether well-fed or hungry, whether living in plenty or in want. I can do all this through him who gives me strength." Our circumstances may change, but we should be steadfast in our connection with God because he does not change.

REFLECTIONS

Our true character emerges not in times of victory but in times of testing. We may need to pull ourselves up and strengthen ourselves in the Lord, just as David did. This vital action allows us to regroup when things are difficult, and the persecution is great. However, if we prepared beforehand we won't be surprised during our testing.

- Injuries or defeats can feel devastating. Yet, in our vulnerabilities, we find God's strength and provision.

- Reflect on a recent challenge and see how God's strength can be or could have been revealed in it.

- Consider a time when you had to rely on other parts of yourself because you were injured or weak. How did you overcome it, and what did you learn about yourself?

ACTION POINTS

Daily Declarations: Speak the Word of God over your life today. Use the scriptures above and declare them over yourself.

Identity Journal: Write out your vulnerabilities, including where you fall short, and ask God to reveal where he comes in to strengthen you.

Community Engagement: Vocalize your process. If you're not feeling well and your teammates don't know, let your family know so they can come in and support you. Hiding your emotions or limitations doesn't help anyone around you, including yourself. Let them in.

Prayer for Finding Strength in Weakness

Lord, thank you for being with us in
our moments of frailty and weakness.
You understand our limitations and
still choose to be with and cover us.
Thank you, God, for revealing your strength
in the center of my weakness.
You're so gracious and kind to us.
Help me embrace your support and love
in addition to the support and love
of people around me. Thank you, God,
that as I'm vulnerable to you,
you will show yourself faithful
and true to me. I honor you.
In Jesus name, amen.

DAY TEN

Teamwork in Christ

"

Ask not what your teammates can do for you; ask what can you do for your teammates.

"

—MAGIC JOHNSON

We all understand team dynamics and how relying on other people is essential to succeeding in any realm of sport. The Bible would describe this as many parts coming together as one. We represent one aspect of God, and we succeed when we work together to serve each other. This mindset actually creates the opportunity for tremendous productivity and success. If we see each other as an integral part of the holistic process, then we will receive each other as valuable and accepted. We will work together to find our commonalities and strive for excellence within each other. This applies to sports and in faith.

More often than not, people are quick to find their differences and dwell on them. Many fail to see that we are more similar and like-minded than we actually believe. Instead of operating out of a negative bias towards one another, where we always look for the thing that we disagree with, or the thing that we find wrong about the other person. We should perceive each other on a base level, the same way that God perceives us. We are made in his image, perhaps with a lot of problems, but nevertheless, we're made to be like him and on the basis of His nature; this is why he loves us. When we are in competition or on teams, even in individual sports. We are only as successful according to our team's effort.

PERCEIVING THE NATURE OF GOD IN OTHERS

Can we perceive the nature of God within the people around us enough to want to be around them? I believe we can. We can look at our peers and see the excellence within them and realize that it is something that we want and care for, because we know if their success is our success. We can celebrate their achievements and partner with them to accomplish great things.

Incorporating God in all that we do is far beyond going to church. We are living life realizing and embracing that God is the God of all of life and not just the God of the church or the God of religion.. He's alive and active in our relationships and as we can perceive him and others, we will partner on an unmatched level in the world around us. We were made to be a part of a team because we need each other. This applies in faith and sport.

SCRIPTURES ON TEAMWORK

The majority of the Bible is about relationships. We see examples of relational failures and relational successes. It's really a blueprint for how we should live our lives. First and foremost, we have the relational dynamics that help us operate with the people around us. The foundational elements of our spiritual journey are also visible, such as how we should connect to God and connect to his spirit. We are given a tremendous invitation within the Word of God. We have all that we need within the Word.

- **Ecclesiastes 4:9-10** - "Two are better than one, because they have a good return for their labor: If either of them falls down, one can help the other up. But pity anyone who falls and has no one to help them up." As much as we'd always like to do things by ourselves because we may feel that we do it better, it is really important to live life with people that you can trust and rely on. This is why team sports are so incredible. It's because we rely on each other to achieve the collaborative end goal which is success and victory.

- **Ephesians 4:16** "states, From him the whole body, joined and held together by every supporting ligament, grows and builds itself up in love, as each part does its work." We must all participate in a growth process because we are interconnected. If someone decides not to grow, then we are all held back by their development or lack thereof.

- **1 Peter 4:8-10** "Above all, keep loving one another earnestly since love covers a multitude of sins. Show hospitality to one another without grumbling. As each has received a gift, use it to serve one another as good stewards of God's varied grace." We are all gifted in the service of others. Our gifts are not just for us, but we have them so we can serve everyone else.

REFLECTIONS

As collaboration and support are vital in and out of competition, our spiritual journey thrives on community and fellowship. We need each other to truly thrive in every environment. Once we realize that we need the person next to us, we'll treat them differently.

- Ask yourself why you need the people around you, pertaining to your emotions, experiences, and growth in faith and competition.

- Think of someone you compete with. Now, identify one thing that you're proud of them for on the field and in their personal life. This will help you see the gold in other people.

- Look for similarities in yourself and the people around you. Once you find something similar, celebrate it.

ACTION POINTS

- **Community Engagement**: Reach out to a teammate or friend in faith. Share an encouragement or pray together for mutual support.
- **Daily Declarations**: Vocalize the gold in other people. The next time you are in a community setting, let the people around you know what you appreciate about them. Now, watch as their relationship with you changes and strengthens.
- **Identity Journal**: Write down ways in which you could be a better team player, practically, emotionally, and spiritually.

Prayer for Teamwork

Lord, I thank you for your demonstration
of teamwork in the Bible. You could have easily
gone out on your own and accomplished
everything you set your heart to,
but you decided to take people with you,
help them, and make them better people.
I thank you that you continue to do this today
in my life. You know that I'm a better person
when I'm around other people, looking at the good
in their lives and helping that come to pass.
Make me a better teammate to my peers,
my friends, and my family.
Thank you, God, for supporting me
in these fundamental aspects of my life.
In Jesus' name, amen

DAY ELEVEN
Leadership Through Service

"

I think that the good and the great are only separated by the willingness to sacrifice.

"

—KAREEM ABDUL-JABBAR

The common understanding of leadership and service is that people in service serve the current leadership. Biblically speaking, the exact opposite would be true. Those in the highest places of leadership are at the bottom, serving everyone else. This is why we see Jesus washing people's feet. The demonstration of true service comes from the bottom. That is why good coaches aren't dictators; they're the most helpful individuals, giving you everything you need to succeed. They go the length to sacrifice and serve for the benefit and betterment of the individual or their teams.

UPSIDE DOWN LEADERSHIP

This upside-down leadership in our own lives is evident when we approach individuals to serve them. We don't come to see what we can get from them but to see what we can give. We don't come to extract or take fame, accolades, or associations from those around us; we come to give what we have. It seems counterintuitive, but this servant mindset gets us much further along in life and with God.

Jesus demonstrated to us the greatest act of leadership known to man. He exposed himself to the broken and poor around him, and instead of condemning them for their failures, he came and served them with love, kindness and sacrifice. This type of leadership undermines control and manipulation, and it emphasizes choice and excellence. When someone serves you with no ulterior motives, how could you not love them? They've shown you what a great leader is actually like. They also exemplify what sacrifice in leadership can look like.

THESE ARE ALL ATTRIBUTES OF JESUS

As you begin to form and shape your leadership style and qualities within yourself, think of areas of support and care. Consider attributes that give instead of extract. Think of ways to guide through love and kindness instead of frustration and anger. Jesus was always anchored in the bigger purpose, and as we entertain the relationships around us, we should also consider them part of a bigger purpose in our lives. This will help us properly prioritize the small things and hold them against the bigger picture of what we hope to achieve and become.

SCRIPTURES ON LEADERSHIP

If God is a servant to us, what should we be to the people around us? We are most definitely not more important or above God, but it's his attitude toward us and his actions toward us that demonstrate authentic love and care. Jesus is always our model for how we should live our lives, and as we glean from these scriptures, we should see that servanthood is a relational path of humility and love.

- **Mark 10:45:** "For even the Son of Man did not come to be served, but to serve, and to give his life as a ransom for many." Jesus provides us with such a great example of servanthood. Did he have to come in service to us? No, he didn't, but he chose to because it's the same way he wants us to live our lives.

- **Hebrews 13:7** says, "Remember your leaders, who spoke the word of God to you. Consider the outcome of their way of life and imitate their faith." We will receive their wisdom and blessings as we let leaders pour into us. True leadership demonstrates a giving and pouring out of the best qualities.

- **Matthew 20:26:** "Not so with you. Instead, whoever wants to become great among you must be your servant." This may seem counterintuitive, but anyone who truly desires to lead is the servant of all because they have laid down any personal agenda for the service of others.

REFLECTIONS

True leadership in sports and faith is exemplified by service and sacrifice, following Jesus' example. Consider times when you give of your time, thoughts, and presence to assist another. This is truly when you become their leader.

- Evaluate your personality and your goals and highlight areas where you serve the best and what you could do better.

- Consider times when you feel like you want to control people or situations and ask yourself why. Once you understand why, look to see if there are ulterior paths to achieving your goal without destroying the people around you.

- Think about the attitude of your head while in an act of service. Is it grateful, thankful, and appreciative, or down, bitter, and resentful?

ACTION POINTS

Daily Declarations: Imitating the faith of others around us is a great way to develop positive mindsets and healthy habits. Identify five people that you would like to reflect to others. fill your mind with who they are and what they're about. What are some things you admire most about their walk with God?

Identity Journal: Write out your leadership style, identifying what you do well and what you see lacking. Give yourself a grade, and come back sometime in the future to take the assessment again.

Community Engagement: Identify one act of service you can perform for your team or community this week.

Prayer for Leadership Through Service

Lord, thank you for showing us what true leadership is actually like. You could have easily come in, taken over, and pushed everyone aside because no one is as perfect and pure as you are. Instead, you submitted yourself before us and before the world and came humbly before us to show us exactly how to lead. We thank you for this sacrificial example of how we should conduct our own relationships. If we truly want to be a great leader, we should lay our lives before others to exalt them to the highest points of their potential. Thank you, God. In Jesus' name, amen.

DAY TWELVE
Integrity On and Off the Field

"

One man practicing sportsmanship is far better than 50 preaching it.

"

—KNUTE ROCKNE

The invisible realities of our lives are visible to everyone, even if we don't know it. Most people think that the people around them do not notice their thoughts, the attitude of their hearts, or even their decisions. This couldn't be further from the truth. The Spiritual world often reflects the physical world. The Bible is very clear on this. The sin of a person searches them out. You can't hide from yourself. This is why we're given clear guidance on how to live our lives and conduct ourselves so that we can be pure from the inside out. Washing the outside of the glass doesn't purify what's inside.

SECRETS ALWAYS COME TO LIGHT

Whatever's done in secret always makes a way to be seen in public at some point. If you mistreat people in the privacy of your own home, it will soon find its way outside of those closed doors. Why? Because someone said something? No, it's because you didn't change, and whoever you are will be manifested everywhere that you show up. This is why we want to live upright and Integris before the Lord. We want to walk in honor and have a moral compass in how we conduct our relationships. This is for your journey of faith and your demeanor as athletes and competitors.

Walking with integrity on and off the field is far more important than just treating people nicely. It's conducting yourself in a way where you're happy with the person that you are becoming and developing into on a daily basis. Because at the end of the day, you have to live with yourself. It's so much easier to conduct life through truthfulness and trustworthiness than to be double-minded in all of our ways. Some believe that they can shortcut the rules in court and in life. If nobody saw it, then nobody's hurt by it, right? The person that is hurt by it is you! You'll be morally depleted if you continually live double-mindedly in all of your ways. You won't like yourself, and you will at one point, express this dislike and hatred in your own body and in the people around you. We are given a road map and a guide on how to live our lives from God, and we need to adhere to it so it can save our souls and actually live the lives he intends for us to live. We are not without hope because we have the redemptive work of Jesus available to us every single day. That's GOOD NEWS!

SCRIPTURE: THE WORD OF GOD IS OUR GUIDE

Through its stories, proverbs, and parables, we're able to establish the shape of who God is to us. Of course, that person expressed in the flesh is Jesus, but we also see his nature throughout the entire Bible. We care very deeply about learning and growing to change our inner world so that we may become the best version of ourselves, not just for the sake of peace in our relationships but because expressing God in our lives or our sports careers is one of the greatest privileges of our lives.

- **Proverbs 11:3** - "The integrity of the upright guides them, but the unfaithful are destroyed by their duplicity." A person filled with integrity walks one path, but someone who is double-minded continually serves multiple masters and is, therefore, doomed to fail. You can't be God's example and the devil sample at the same time.

- **Proverbs 10:9** says, "Whoever walks in integrity walks securely, but whoever takes crooked paths will be found out." The foundation of a person with integrity is truth. You can stand on the truth because the truth will always set you free. Crooked paths lead to unexpected outcomes. This analogy goes into every area of our Lives, including our relationships and our practices. It also transfers over into your habits and behaviors as an athlete.

- **Proverbs 2:6-7** "For the LORD gives wisdom, from his mouth come knowledge and understanding. He holds success in store for the upright; he is a shield to those whose walk is blameless." God invests heavily in those who walk upright and prioritize truth and purity. He releases wisdom; for those who accept it, he is their shield. Wisdom is not merely about how much you know but also how much you are willing to surrender.

REFLECTIONS

The invisible parts of who we are guide us in everything that we do. Consider your actions and how they affect you. Maybe you're too harsh on some people, or you ignore others. Ask yourself, What feelings and thoughts are you harboring to develop these actions?

- Your character and integrity in sports reflect your commitment to Christ and your craft. Choose honesty and integrity in every action. It will overflow in all areas of your life.

- Reflect on an area where you're tempted to compromise your integrity. Commit to making an honorable choice. And tell someone to hold you accountable.

- Evaluate your heart and work on changing 1% today to make better internal decisions. Ask God what should be added or subtracted out of your life.

ACTION POINTS

Daily Declarations: Meditate on the word as it will change and transform who you are. Pick three scriptures today to focus on that pertain to your integrity.

Identity Journal: Be honest with yourself. Journal about decisions that you felt compromised your ability to be the best version of yourself. Your honesty is the amount you're willing to change.

Community Engagement: Go back into your past and let the people around you know when you let them down and weren't walking in integrity and how you won't do it again. This will remove the burden and open up a time for healing and repair. It will be a challenging step but one of the most empowering ones at the same time.

Prayer for Integrity

Lord, thank you for showing us what it's like to
walk on the Earth with integrity and righteousness.
You show us what it's like to have firm boundaries
and have a purpose that you live towards.
You care more about our inner world than about
the things around us or our material possessions.
Thank you, God, for valuing the attitude of our
hearts and our thoughts more than most things.
Help us to perceive your heart and your mind for
the moral compass that we're building in our lives.
Help us to walk with integrity in all that we do.
Thank you, Jesus. In Jesus name, amen.

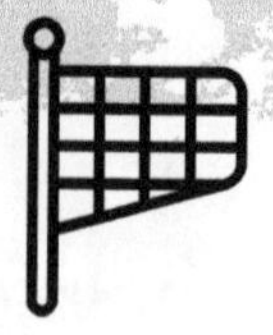

DAY THIRTEEN

Perseverance Through Trials

“

I've missed more than 9000 shots in my career. I've lost almost 300 games. 26 times, I've been trusted to take the game-winning shot and missed. I've failed over and over and over again in my life. And that is why I succeed.

”

—MICHAEL JORDAN

There's nothing like performing your best when you're feeling great; everything's going smoothly. Unfortunately, that's not the case all the time. We are constantly in situations where we have to push through and persevere amid our obstacles and our trials. It seems at times that the world doesn't care about us; it just continues to spin. Or we're just looking for a break because it's been unrelenting. I know many of you can relate to this. Even though we plan for things to go well, sometimes situations change our approach. Because of this, we need to have perseverance and the ability to fight and push through.

It seems to be inevitable that we will have trials and testing as we grow and develop in life. That's competition, isn't it? Sports, the majority of the time, serve as an active test of endurance, skill, and determination. This testing, though, actually refines us in a way. It makes us stronger, faster, wiser. Perhaps trials and tribulations are always part of our plan for growth. It's almost guaranteed that we will face different obstacles in each season of life, but it's certainly guaranteed that you will face opposition in competition as you progress as an athlete.

We are fast-tracking our growth strategy by going through moments of testing for our mind, emotions, and body. It's essential that we find a way to persevere through these tests. For what doesn't break us only makes us stronger is more true than we think it is. With each and every test, we increase our capacity, our grace, and our skills. It's like shooting a basketball; with practice consistently, you will become better. There's nothing greater than feeling a physical test in your mind with emotions simultaneously, and you have the fortitude to push through. That is the test of our lives played out in sports every day as well as our faith.

Perseverance is a common theme in the Old and New Testament in the bible. We only persevere through the things that we value. We are invited to develop an internal fortitude, a reservoir of sorts, to draw from in times of need and trials. It is said in modern times to dig deep in your gut and fight and push through the pain. As we reach these pinnacle moments, the outcomes always change us because we believe in ourselves more. Also, we see the depths of our faith deepen in knowing the faithfulness of God. We can now see the evidence of our belief and our work, which is truly remarkable. The more you are willing to put the work in for your craft, the more you will see the results. This is the same with faith. God will be as good to you as the depth in which you are willing to explore Him!

SCRIPTURES ON PERSEVERANCE

One of the most monumental stories in the Bible is when Jesus subjected himself to being tested with every temptation under the sun. He proved to be victorious and showed us exactly what it's like to be rightly submitted to God and empowered to push through the trials before him. There are countless stories of perseverance because we are blessed when we persevere. The testing actually proves us to be stronger and purer.

- **James 1:12** - "Blessed is the one who perseveres under trial because, having stood the test, that person will receive the crown of life that the Lord has promised to those who love him."

- **Philippians 1:19-21**, "for I know that this will turn out for my deliverance through your prayers and the provision of the Spirit of Jesus Christ, according to my earnest expectation and hope, that I will not be put to shame in anything, but that with all boldness, Christ will even now, as always, be exalted in my body, whether by life or by death. For to me, to live is Christ, and to die is gain."

- **Galatians 6:9:** "And let us not grow weary of doing good, for in due season we will reap if we do not give up."

REFLECTIONS

Challenges in athletics can cultivate endurance and character, mirroring our spiritual trials that strengthen our faith. It truly is incredible how versatile athletics is and how it trains our personal lives. Don't underestimate moments in practice or in competition because they are, in fact, developing you as an individual.

- Consider a recent trial. How can you see it as an opportunity for spiritual growth?

- What are moments in your life when you would be most proud of yourself? They are likely tied to some obstacle.

- Recall a time in life when you gave more than you thought you had. Where did the extra effort come from, and how can you access that now? What were you feeling at the time?

ACTION POINTS

Daily Declarations: Continue to speak over yourself before a trial, especially when you're in one. Recalling scripture to emphasize the reward set before you is exactly what God wants you to do.

Identity Journal: Process vulnerably in writing ways in which you feel like you are proud of yourself for persevering in the past. Even if you didn't complete the task at hand, did you do better than you thought you would have?

Community Engagement: Testing is a great way to grow. What better activity than to test yourself through difficult practice? Don't seek comfort when you want greatness. Reach out to people who are better than you in your particular sport and practice with them. Pick their brain on how they push through to persevere.

Prayer for Perseverance Through Trials

Lord, thank you that you helped us
like Shadrach Meshach and Abednego.
You were with them in the midst of the fire.
You help us to push through trials, obstacles,
and momentary light affliction.
You are a strong tower that we can lean on.
You give us sufficient grace for every moment of
our life, and we do not have one want or need
because of the grace you provide.
We lack nothing because we're with you.
We will remain steadfast in you because
you remain steadfast in us. Thank you, God,
for never giving up on us.
In Jesus name, amen.

DAY FOURTEEN
Sharing Your Faith Story

"

The most important thing is to try and inspire people so that they can be great in whatever they want to do.

"

—KOBE BRYANT

We don't fully know the impact that sharing our story will have with others. Everyone's on their own faith journey. Some are at the very beginning, and others are more seasoned. However, we don't fully know where everyone else is around us. They may be in complete opposition to everything that we say and do, and that's okay. Moreover, they may be in total support of who we are and what we're about, but we might not know it because we haven't yet taken the time to openly share our faith journey.

People are often surprised and don't know that their friends and peers have their own faith journeys. But these announcements are met with tremendous celebration because now, not only do you have a physical life to live with this individual, but you also have an everlasting life. This broadens our collaboration's scope and impact today and in the future. It also gives us a ton of additional areas to relate to our peers.

Sharing your story about where you started and where you are now doesn't make you an evangelist. It makes you a real person. It doesn't even make you spiritual; it makes you genuine and authentic. If God truly helped you and you share that experience with others, aren't you giving them the greatest gift that you've received? You're being a good friend to them by letting them know about this great God. That makes you helpful and relatable in times when they may be in distress. Try not to over-spiritualize it. It's easy for someone to measure the fruit of your life, and it's your job to show it. When others see your success in sports, they will ask you how you got there. Which gives you the opportunity to talk about the grind of putting the work in. It's the same with your faith journey.

One of the greatest reasons we would want to open up and share our journey or our testimony with those around us is because it will illuminate a path available to them. Perhaps you started your faith journey in tremendous opposition, where you were running away from God and hurting people with your actions, and you turned around completely. Now, you've given your life to help others. Not only does this give them a blueprint for how they could respond if they see themselves in your past, but it also gives them an invitation to get to know God in a tremendous way that they may never have heard before. As we share our story with others we are inviting God in the midst to testify how powerful and loving he is. All of Heaven is truly celebrating when we share our testimony.

SCRIPTURES ON SHARING YOUR FAITH

The consideration of sharing your faith will bring up many emotions because your faith journey is tied to many emotional experiences. Take comfort in your purpose rather than in your insecurities! The scriptures will guide you in this process because there is a higher calling when we share our testimony. At the end of the day, it's not about us; it's about them and always about Him!

- **1 Peter 3:15** - "But in your hearts revere Christ as Lord. Always be prepared to give an answer to everyone who asks you to give the reason for the hope that you have. But do this with gentleness and respect."

- **2 Timothy 1:8-12** Do not be ashamed, then, of witnessing for our Lord; neither be ashamed of me, a prisoner for Christ's sake. Instead, take your part in suffering for the good news, as God gives you the strength for it. He saved us and called us to be his own people, not because of what we have done, but because of his own purpose and grace. He gave us this grace by means of Christ Jesus before the beginning of time, but now it has been revealed to us through the coming of our Savior, Christ Jesus. He has ended the power of death and, through the gospel, has revealed immortal life.

- **Matthew 5:14-16** "You are like light for the whole world. A city built on a hill cannot be hidden. No one lights a lamp and puts it under a bowl; instead, it is put on the lampstand, where it gives light to everyone in the house. In the same way, your light must shine before people so that they will see the good things you do and praise your Father in heaven."

REFLECTION

As an athlete, your platform can be a powerful tool for sharing your hope and faith in Christ. It doesn't need to be a manufactured testimony. As long as you're being authentic and true to yourself and sharing what you feel comfortable with, then it could be a great thing.

- Prepare a brief testimony of your faith journey. Look for an opportunity to share it this week amongst your environment. Team, family, coaches, etc.

- Consider breaking up elements of your past to highlight easily understood and comfortable testimonies you'd like to share.

- It's okay if you're still on a healing journey or growing in your faith. You don't have to share everything. Ask yourself what you feel comfortable discussing that God has done in your life openly. Because talking openly involves a level of responsibility.

ACTION POINTS

Daily Declarations: Remind yourself of what the scriptures say about who you are. You are not your past because your past was bought with a price. Ask God to tell you who you are. Who do you say that I am?

Identity Journal: It's a really great idea to write out your testimony in a few different ways. One way you could write it out is for the most amount of people to hear it. How could you tell your story so it doesn't exclude anyone, like someone who's young or someone who has no clue about Jesus at all? Additionally, you can write out your faith journey as if you were talking to a church or your friends in the locker room. Look at incorporating scriptures that speak to you to help you become more comfortable sharing.

Community Engagement: Different settings will provide different opportunities. Consider sharing your story openly to those around you and highlighting the benefits of what you've received from God. As long as you're authentic and genuine, you shouldn't this will empower you to be bold in sharing your story. Some like to simply thank God in public as an introductory means to sharing their faith. That's a great idea if that's where you want to start.

Prayer for Faith to Share

Lord, thank you for sharing your story with us.
You opened up your heart and your mind,
and you shared the story of humanity with us
in the Bible. You are transparent in your emotions
and your victories and difficulties. God, thank you
for allowing us to see you in such a vulnerable state.
Give us the strength to share our own story.
First, so that our fear and our failures would not
limit us but that we would be open to testifying
of your goodness before and after. Give us the
words to speak so that we may glorify you.
Thank you, Lord. In Jesus Name, Amen.

DAY FIFTEEN
The Importance of Rest

"

To give any less than your best is to sacrifice a gift.

"

—STEVE PREFONTAINE

Our bodies were made to rest each and every day and more in certain seasons of life. This is the frailty of our nature: We need to stop in order to rejuvenate. In a minor way, we see how it's healthy in the midst of competitive sports to stop and take a break, catch our breath, and get some water. We weren't made to be like machines that can run 24 hours a day, seven days a week, as much as we'd like to believe that we are.

TIME TO LAY DOWN

One of the first things that God did in the Book of Genesis was to lay Adam down in order to create Eve from Adam's place of rest. This is a vital thing to know because we are often able to create and rejuvenate our minds, bodies, and emotions when we rest. We're all familiar with how cells break down when we exercise and how they need time to rejuvenate. The same thing happens with our minds. In addition to the repair process that takes place in our muscles, we also have to give our bodies enough time to remove all of the extra waste from our caloric burn. This is why we feel like we have brain fog if we don't sleep enough.

SPIRITUAL WELL-BEING IS TIED TO REST

Our spiritual and emotional well-being is also tied to physical rest. If we're running around the void of good sleep, our emotions will be taxed, and our sense of self and well-being will be diminished. Also, it impacts your ability to perform in competition when your body does not have the proper amount of rest. We won't think very highly of ourselves because we feel exhausted and burdened. The interconnected parts of our body are spoken about in the book of Hebrews, and we need to train ourselves and not neglect any part because they impact each other.

Rest is possible first in our hearts. The visible signs of rest are often seen when we slow down and limit movement. However, rest is truly an attitude of the heart. Of course, we need to slow down sometimes and nap, but more importantly, if we can train ourselves to rest, then we know our limits and the best things to do to maximize our productivity while maintaining a high value on our spirit, soul, and body.

SCRIPTURES ON REST

The scriptures in the Bible on rest often give us an invitation to rely on God when we are weary. It's easy to see the different examples in the Old and New Testament when people got to the end of themselves and they are only left with the option to choose God. We all need rest from our work. Go to Jesus, who will give you rest.

- **Mark 6:31** - "Then, because so many people were coming and going that they did not even have a chance to eat, he said to them, 'Come with me by yourselves to a quiet place and get some rest.'" The importance of this verse is to recognize the need to separate from the crowd sometimes and go to a quiet place. The lack of activity and decrease in noise is a sufficient environment to rejuvenate your mind, will, and emotions.

- **Matthew 11:28** “Come to me, all you who are weary and burdened, and I will give you rest.” This is a direct invitation from God for those that feel burdened to go to him and he will exchange rest for whatever you are burdened by. Remember this verse when you feel down and exhausted, Jesus has rest for you if you desire it.

- **Matthew 11:29:** “Take my yoke upon you and learn from me, for I am gentle and humble in heart, and you will find rest for your souls.” God’s yoke is light, and sometimes ours is heavy. If we receive his yoke from him, it will be gentle and provide us rest. In this verse, it’s also important to note that God wants to supply rest for our souls. It could also be said if you don’t have Jesus, your soul is not able to rest.

REFLECTIONS

Rest is vital for physical and spiritual renewal. Jesus Himself modeled the balance of work and rest. Rest must be understood within the context of humanity. If we embrace it as the Bible requests, then we will see its reward, and we won’t fight it because we feel like we’re not doing something productive. As important as it is to rest as an athlete to be able to perform at peak performance, it’s just as important to have rest in your spiritual life.

- Plan a time this week to rest from athletics and other activities and focus instead on quiet time with God. Pray, read, and reflect on God’s presence in your life.

- Consider times of contemplation when you play very little music or are completely silent. Take note of how much rest it gives you. Do you feel more rested?

- Consider within yourself the voice that's in your head. How loud is that voice speaking to you on a regular basis? Typically, the louder the voice, the more evidence there is that you are not listening to it.

ACTION POINTS

Get out: Take some time this week to go for a walk. Listen to your thoughts and try to quiet your mind. Keep track of how this makes you feel because it's often a reflection of your inner world.

Identity Journal: Journal the limitations you feel right now about why you're not able to relax. Write down all of your reasons. Now, ask God if he's big enough to answer every reason and provide you with rest.

Community Engagement: Break away from the grind and go see a movie or go to a quiet space in your home or in your city and sit in peace, thanking God for rest. It's amazing how many people forego self-care for other rewards. Invite someone to go out with you to relax if you feel led to have company.

Prayer for Rest

Lord, thank you for showing us exactly
what it means to rest in you. Even when
you could have worked more, tried to talk
to more people, or performed more miracles,
you found it fitting to rest in the midst
of the work. This was to give us an example of
how to rest during the everyday grind of life.
Lord, we want that for our own lives.
We want to be an example of who you are
in the midst of being busy. We trust in you.
We know that rest rejuvenates our bodies,
minds, emotions, and spirit. Thank you, God,
for giving us tools that help us succeed in life,
and please remind us when we need to rest.
In Jesus name, amen.

DAY SIXTEEN

The Role of Humility

“

The only way to prove that you're a good sport is to lose.

”

—ERNIE BANKS

There's a pathway available to us in life that God often wants us to choose. It's the path of humility. When we humble ourselves before God and man, we display a submission to God that attracts heaven. Humility and competition are not often linked together, at times, in fact it's considered a form of weakness by some in sports. Yet this trait requires a sense of self-confidence in God, not cockieness in ourselves. It's truly an attitude of the heart that's displayed through our actions. Our behavior before others can be cultivated in our posture before God.

PREFERRING OTHERS ON AND OFF THE FIELD

If you were to simply define humility, it would be preferring others over yourself. This idea is so attractive to God that he asked you to be clothed in it. He knows that you'll be covered and will be on the path to success when you prefer others over yourself. So many see what's possible in life and sacrifice everybody in their way in order to achieve it. This is what the world would tell you to do. The opposite would be the case in the Kingdom of God. You don't sacrifice others so that you can receive your upgrade. You serve them, and out of your humble heart, in the prioritization of others, you're able to receive your upgrade. This principle is true of successful athletes and teams as well. They pride themselves on going above and beyond for each other in order to obtain the ultimate prize of success and victory.

The opposite of humility is pride, which will destroy anything in its path. Pride was the fall of the devil (Lucifer), who was a worshiping angel in the presence of God. Pride will try to convince you that you don't need God. In an effort for us to be protected, God asked us to take on humanity because he knows it will serve us well. God knows exactly what will happen if you fill yourself with pride, so he automatically opposes it. It's time for us to realize the power of humility and how it actually creates a magnetic attraction of success in your lives and careers.

SCRIPTURES ON HUMILITY

Every scripture on humility speaks of our hearts' nature and the byproduct of our efforts. If we can walk in humility, then we'll be favored by God. This is an interconnected way for us to love and prefer others to keep humanity going. God knows that when people have humility, our communities thrive.

- **Philippians 2:3-4** - "Do nothing out of selfish ambition or vain conceit. Rather, in humility, value others above yourselves, not looking to your own interests but each of you to the interests of the others." Selfish ambition is the root of destructive things not only for ourselves but for the people around us. If we automatically value putting others above ourselves, we will guard our hearts and minds from self-destruction.

- **Colossians 3:12** "Therefore, as God's chosen people, holy and dearly loved, clothe yourselves with compassion, kindness, humility, gentleness and patience." The imagery here of putting on God's attributes as our clothes is profound. Imagine getting dressed with humility. If you don't put it on, then you're walking around naked, exposed to the elements. Consider the comprehensive nature of getting dressed in something every day. Humility is not some small matter; it's a lifestyle.

- **James 4:6** But he gives us more grace. That is why scripture says, "God opposes the proud but shows favor to the humble." Scripture often presents us with opposition to a matter. It can be really good for us to know what God hates and what God despises. Pride is the opposite of humility, and God opposes the proud. Pride can also diminish your probability of winning as it's self focused and not team focused. Let that sink in.

REFLECTIONS

Humility allows us to see the value in others and acknowledges our need for God's strength and wisdom. It also protects our hearts from going astray and thinking that the victories and successes we've had in life are solely because of our own hands and not because of God's doing.

- In your interactions today, consciously put others first, whether in conversation, training, or competition.

- Consider how humility affects your mind and your heart. Do you feel more love when you approach situations with humility rather than pride?

- Think back on the last time that you chose to be proud instead of humble. How did that affect you and your relationships?

ACTION POINTS

Daily Declarations: Praying scripture over yourself is a great way to declare your intention with God. Think of different situations in your life right now that you can pray over and declare the nature of God for yourself.

Identity Journal: Evaluating your heart in journaling is an extremely important task for measuring your relationship with God and personal development. Write down different situations and how you chose to respond. What outcomes did you perceive to be desirable, and which ones didn't turn out so well? Ask yourself, what attributes were you wearing that day?

Community Engagement: Humility is best described as the preferential treatment of others. It is so easy to be a kind and humble person and to take actions that favor others. Nothing is more desirable than a humble friend who takes care of others. Make humility a lifestyle decision; you will be rewarded for it.

Prayer for Humility

Lord, thank you for showing us what
it's like to live a life humbly before God
and man. You teach us that the path is narrow
and requires us to be humble. Just as we are to go
through the narrow gate and offload our baggage.
Teach us to seek humility over being proud.
We know that an inheritance is available
for those who are Meek and humble.
Thank you, God, for showing us the path of
righteousness and grace. We love you, Jesus.
In Jesus' name, amen

DAY SEVENTEEN

Cultivating Spiritual Discipline

"

If you can't outplay them, outwork them.

"

—BEN HOGAN

Discipline has been the foundational cornerstone for every form of athletics since the beginning. If one is not committed to sticking with a routine and a regiment and practicing repeatedly, how could one possibly be good at something in the long run? We know how much discipline matters to success. It's actually impossible to see long-term success without tremendous discipline. Even the best in the world still need to apply themselves in order to cultivate their craft. Discipline also helps develop tenure in sports and faith.

For most of our lives, we've measured discipline as showing up, practicing, and pushing through. However, before it's an action, it's an attitude of the heart and a mindset of one desiring victory. Yet some people don't desire it or understand the commitment of this principle. This same discipline should be applied to our spiritual lives as well. We know that we can achieve success when we have discipline in a craft. The same would apply to spiritual discipline. It's like a measured commitment to God. The more we commit to him and show up, the more access we receive from God.

The big revelation here is that we don't consider God, and our access to God is limited only when we're in need. Many people find God in their time of need, which is a wonderful thing. However, they don't have an active relationship to go off of because they only seek him when they have a need. Imagine a relationship built only around needs. It's one-sided and not very fruitful because there's no collaboration or mutual contribution. How could you trust someone if they only come to you when they need it? This is why our active relationship with God requires cultivating "spiritual discipline". We don't want to be out of a relationship with God. We want him to be ever more present in our lives. Not only do we want to demonstrate our care and prioritization of God's heart, but we also want to apply ourselves so that we can become the very best individuals possible.

As we begin to cultivate spiritual discipline in our lives, we realize that we are spirit first before we ever were in the flesh. And if you believe in God and accept Jesus as your savior, then you will have everlasting life with him. This means your spiritual journey starts today and will continue to the day you go to heaven. If we plan on spending eternity with God, then why would we live our lives in a way that ignores him today? Kind of silly, right? The available spiritual discipline is far greater than what you may find inside the church or just on Sunday gatherings. This spiritual discipline is for you daily; no institution or person can cultivate spiritual discipline for you. You have to take responsibility for your hunger to be disciplined in your craft and your faith.

SCRIPTURES ON CULTIVATING SPIRITUAL DISCIPLINE

What truly matters to God is your relationship with him. It's not about the appearance of what you do or what you don't do, as many would like to believe. Your dedicated commitment to God demonstrated through spiritual discipline, is one of the most important things in your life. Scripture allows us to define our pursuit so that we may find God.

- **1 Timothy 4:7-8** - "Have nothing to do with godless myths and old wives' tales; rather, train yourself to be godly. Physical training is valuable, but godliness has value for all things, holding promise for both the present life and the life to come." The importance of the scripture is to not diminish physical activity but rather compare it to godliness. The reason why godliness is prioritized and valued significantly higher than physical training is that it carries into our everlasting life. But it also transfers over to the skills we are developing not only in sport but in faith.

- **Matthew 6:16–18:** “And when you fast, do not look gloomy like the hypocrites, for they disfigure their faces that their fasting may be seen by others. Truly, I say to you, they have received their reward. But when you fast, anoint your head, and wash your face, your fasting may not be seen by others but by your Father, who is in secret. And your Father who sees in secret will reward you.” There is a difference between religion and relationship. Religion would tell you to perform for others and make the appearance look like you have tremendous spiritual discipline. Active relationships wouldn’t care if anyone knows about your relationship at all. Your commitment should be for God solely.

- **2 Timothy 3:16–17:** “All Scripture is breathed out by God and profitable for teaching, for reproof, for correction, and for training in righteousness, that the man of God may be complete, equipped for every good work.” We plan our training in life, and anytime we apply ourselves to the word of God, we are training ourselves in righteousness. This is the definition of Heaven’s spiritual discipline because we want to be equipped in every good work available to us.

REFLECTIONS

Just as you commit to physical training, spiritual discipline is crucial for growth and maturity in your faith. Once we realize that God wants an active relationship with us, the relational dynamics are evaluated. Can you show up for God and show the commitment, love, and sacrifice that he requires? This is spiritual discipline walked out.

- Consider the elements that you find missing in your relationship with God and ask yourself why.
- What are some ways that you are training yourself up and righteousness this week?
- Is there someone around you who has a dedicated spiritual discipline from which you would like to glean?

ACTION POINTS

Daily Discipline: Identify one spiritual discipline (prayer, fasting, service) to focus on developing this week.

Identity Journal: Write out three things today that you want to improve in your spiritual discipline with God. It could be a measurement of time that you commit to spending with him, a small change in your daily devotions, or listening to a sermon or a podcast during your free time.

Community Engagement: Praying before every game or practice is a really good discipline. Consider starting your next game with prayer, and if you feel inclined, invite others to join you. Remember people will desire your results, but will be more blessed to understand your discipline behind those results.

Prayer for Spiritual Discipline

Lord, thank you for teaching us spiritual discipline not only to physically ourselves but also to develop a relational process to grow with you. You show up for us daily and help us mature in our faith and journey. Thank you for the fortitude and the foundation to build and grow on everything that you've provided for us. You are training us for righteousness. I respond to you by showing up and participating because I know it is a focus on you. My path will become illuminated, and my way will become great. Thank you, Jesus.
In Jesus name, amen.

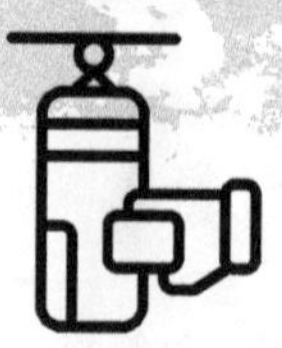

DAY EIGHTEEN
Overcoming Temptation

"

I hated every minute of training, but I said, 'Don't quit. Suffer now and live the rest of your life as a champion.

"

—MUHAMMAD ALI

The temptations in life seem plentiful. Everyday as the world progresses it seems like we have more temptations surrounding us. Whether we're tempted to break our commitments or overextend ourselves, there's really no limit to the amount of temptations available. So what do we do in the face of such adversity? We must apply ourselves to a self-control that harnesses the values that we have in life.

We must seek guidance and support from God so that we can have the inner strength to hold steadfast to what we care so deeply about. We must see the temptation as an opportunity for inner strength and a test for us to prove who we are and who we are not. Temptations are the proving ground for those who want access to God. If we see them as obstacles that we can overcome, which they are, then we won't treat them any more than a test that we need to pass. What if Temptations were here so that we could prove ourselves to God as faithful and true? They just might be used as a pivotal cornerstone to our faith.

The choice is truly yours. Will you be tossed back and forth by the Temptations of life, or will you cultivate the gift of self-control that you've been given and prioritize the things that are truly important to you and to God? Will you be able to prove yourself holy and blameless before God through your commitment to persevere in the face of adversity? What other options do we have to overcome?

The rewards for those who overcome them are great and worth it. You might not know that you are an overcomer.

SCRIPTURES ON OVERCOMING TEMPTATION

Once you pull the veil back on temptation, you realize how common it actually is. There would be a misconception about its uniqueness to you. You are not special in this regard. All temptations are common to mankind. Furthermore, God has given you all the power to overcome them. The option is truly yours.

- **1 Corinthians 10:13:** "No temptation has overtaken you except what is common to mankind. And God is faithful; he will not let you be tempted beyond what you can bear. But when you are tempted, he will also provide a way out so that you can endure it." This verse is the definition of a test. God will ensure that you're not tempted beyond what you can bear, and he will provide you with a way out when you are tempted. Every temptation is a test of your heart, mind, and will.

- **James 1:13-14:** "No one undergoing a trial should say, 'I am being tempted by God,' since God is not tempted by evil, and he himself doesn't tempt anyone. But each person is tempted when he is drawn away and enticed by his own evil desire." (CSB) The origin of temptation is important for us to know. We may be tempted, thinking it could be from God, but that is not the case. God May permit something, but that doesn't mean he's the creator of it.

- **Luke 4:13:** "And when the devil had ended every temptation, he departed from him until an opportune time." (ESV) We should never forget that Jesus endured every temptation known to man. He proved himself to be faithful and true and did not waiver in the midst of all of these temptations. He knew we needed a perfect and true example, and we have that in Jesus.

REFLECTIONS

Temptations can derail even the strongest athletes. Remember, God provides strength and a way to stand firm. Once we receive a measure of success, it seems as though the temptations will increase. This is why we need to have a firm foundation with God so that when we grow in life and succeed in different areas, we can stand firm on solid ground.

- Think back on your last temptation. Without getting too introspective, what does it say about you? How did it get a hold of your attention?

- Consider the temptations that you've already overcome something in your past that you have not been tempted by in a long time. What did you do differently that made that switch?

- Can you see the people around you and the temptations they are falling into? Tread with caution because temptations love to reproduce.

ACTION POINTS

Daily Declarations: With every temptation, there's a way out. The next time you feel even mildly tempted, run in the opposite direction. Declare to yourself who God says you are instead of falling for it.

Identity Journal: Face today's challenges with the confidence that God will provide a way through them—Journal about the experience. Also, acknowledge the challenge and what you feel God wants you to see in the situation.

Community Engagement: Our environment sometimes dictates the level of temptation that we experience. If you know that you will be tempted if you go to certain events, concerts, or establishments, then why would you go? The next time you're presented with the idea of participating in these environments, communicate out loud that this would infringe on your boundaries and your values. Instead, plan times and environments where you know you're guaranteed to have a successful experience.

Prayer for Overcoming Temptation

Lord, I thank you for never allowing us to
be in a situation that we don't have the grace
to overcome. You alone showed us what it's like
to endure persistent, overwhelming temptation,
and you didn't give in. You allowed yourself
to be subjected to the very same things that we
experience, but you overcame it.
We trust you to continue to supply the grace
necessary for us to overcome as well.
We know that you are with us, and we are
not alone. Thank you for allowing us to
be vulnerable to you and to strengthen us
in our time of weakness.
In Jesus name, amen.

DAY NINETEEN
The Power of a Positive Attitude

"

Success is not the key to happiness.
Happiness is the key to success.
If you love what you are doing,
you will be successful.

"

—ALBERT SCHWEITZER

How many times have you been in an environment where someone walks in with a bad attitude? Have you ever noticed how it brings down the entire room or your team? Our personal attitudes not only manifest in what we say but also in what we do. It's nearly impossible to hide our thoughts from our actions. Now, imagine you're trying to prepare for a big game. Your mental energy needs to be pointed toward the success of the game. You need to have optimism, hope, and strategy in your mind. If you don't and you're distracted, you won't be on your A game.

POSITIVITY IS AN ATTITUDE, LIFESTYLE, AND CHOICE.

The power of positivity and a positive attitude is incredible when it comes to our minds, will, and emotions. People will believe more in us if we come to support them with an upright and positive attitude. This will create more continuity within our relationships. In addition, it's the mental posture that looks ahead toward the future, which is the goal set before you manifest it. People who demonstrate positive thinking see the value in synergy and in their investment.

THINGS MAY STILL GO WRONG

Having a positive attitude doesn't mean that things won't go wrong. Of course, they will. However, if you have a positive attitude and things go wrong, then they don't derail you as often or as deeply as they may have if you were to be pessimistic about everything. People who refuse to have a positive attitude hang on to unforgiveness and bitterness longer. Unforgiveness and bitterness make us unproductive and unsuccessful. The power of positivity is not just wishful thinking. It's an attitude of the heart that's manifested in our actions. It also transfers over into our life skills and communication.

SCRIPTURES ON POSITIVE ATTITUDES

The Bible is clear on positivity and the attitudes of our hearts. We are consistently invited into the checks and balances of what we carry in our hearts. The evaluation is good because it will keep you focusing on the right things and inviting the right things into your heart in mind.

- **Philippians 4:8** - "Finally, brothers and sisters, whatever is true, whatever is noble, whatever is right, whatever is pure, whatever is lovely, whatever is admirable—if anything is excellent or praiseworthy—think about such things." Dwelling on what is good not only sets our mood but it also sets our mind in the right direction, and when our mind is pointed in the right direction, we can accomplish great things.

- **1 Thessalonians 5:16** Rejoice always. NIV: This passage makes the point very clearly: Scripture is an invitation, but it's also a commandment. If we rejoice always, our hearts will be pointed in the right direction, and we will welcome what is ahead of us and not be limited by our past.

- **Romans 5:3-4** "Not only so, but we also glory in our sufferings, because we know that suffering produces perseverance; perseverance, character; and character, hope." NIV In Romans 5, we see that there's a process in life to self-development. This process provides us with hope because even the things that we're going through, including suffering, are helping us shape the better person that we're becoming.

REFLECTIONS

A positive mindset, rooted in Christ's promises, can transform your approach to competition, training, and life. How can we achieve something that we've never done before without believing in it, hoping for it, and desiring it? The entire landscape of competition is separated by people who can think ahead and those who look behind.

- Consider one mindset that you have that feeds into a positive process. How does it assist you?

- Reflect on people in your life who typically don't have a good attitude. Ask yourself why so you can understand the dynamics that feed into their mood. Also so you can guard from allowing that to impact you.

- Reflect and recall the promises in God's word that speak highly of who you are. Ask yourself what God calls you. He also talks about having an appropriate attitude, even during tough times.

ACTION POINTS

Daily Declarations: Before your next practice or game, meditate on 1 Thessalonians 5:16, focusing on the positive. Take note of how it impacted your performance and attitude.

Identity Journal: Write out everything you love about yourself. It may seem weird to do but it's really helpful for you to remind yourself about all the things that you like about yourself. This is not a self-deprecating exercise, but it is to help build your confidence. The bible says: "Love thy neighbor as you love yourself"

Community Engagement: The next time you meet as a group within your family or your team, show up with an overly positive mindset. Notice how it changes the room and the people around you.

Prayer for the Power of a Positive Attitude

Lord, thank you for showing us
the power of positive thinking. You ask us
to set our minds on the above things, which will
guide us. We know that as we adopt the mind of
Christ for ourselves, we will not only replace our
bad mindsets but also focus on the good, the pure,
and the righteous way in which you'd like us to be.
Help us to hold steadfast in being a light that
shines on Hill with our mindsets and our words.
Help us to be known for our positivity and our love.
Thank you, Jesus, amen.

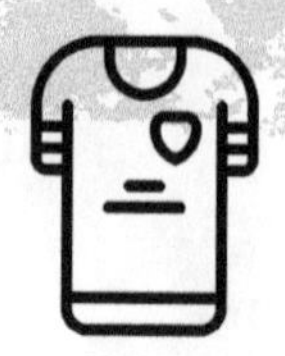

DAY TWENTY

Faith as the Foundation of Team Unity

“

Individual commitment to a group effort – that is what makes a team work, a company work, a society work, a civilization work.

”

—VINCE LOMBARDI

As a team gathers together, they look for a common purpose. In some sports, it's the championship game at the end of the season. Perhaps it's to go undefeated and to accomplish personal levels of success. Each team has common goals they want to accomplish, and they do that by establishing core values. Some of the best coaches make it a point to establish a purpose in a calling beyond their sport's practicalities. Why do they do this? It's because they know if people can connect on a deep spiritual level, they will be more unified and accomplish greater things.

FAITH PROVIDES CONNECTION

Let's take basketball, for example. You can learn how to shoot the basketball better and defend better, but if you don't have team unity, that dysfunction will play out in the game. There's an unlimited number of ways that this dysfunction can keep us from truly succeeding. How do we overcome this? We need to have a higher purpose that we tie our actions too. In our spiritual journey, faith is the cornerstone of our foundation. Faith gives us the merit to believe in something we have not yet achieved.

ACCESSING GOD

Faith not only provides us with the opportunity to access God, but the Bible clearly says that we don't have access to God without faith. Faith is also the invitation for God to join our present activities. We are inviting him into our day. This invitation should go out beyond ourselves and into our entire team because when we are working for God and working with him, then everything we put our hands to do should be blessed by him. If we're not acting on our own presumption or strength but coordinating our team around our faith in God, then our hearts will be pointed in the right direction, and we will see more of him as we compete.

Many have said that believing is seeing what you hope for. Faith is the same way. If we can coordinate our faith as a team to believe in great things, then the unity we will experience will be deep and profound. We might accomplish everything set in our hearts if we can build and collaborate around our faith in God.

SCRIPTURES ON FAITH AND UNITY

God places great emphasis on Unity in the Bible. He desperately hopes that we achieve synergy because he knows we're limited without it. We have the exact same spiritual disciplines, including faith, at our disposal to get us there.

- **1 Corinthians 1:10:** "I appeal to you, brothers and sisters, in the name of our Lord Jesus Christ, that all of you agree with one another in what you say and that there be no divisions among you, but that you be perfectly united in mind and thought." Divisions not only separate us physically, but they separate us spiritually and emotionally. This is what we see in 1 Corinthians 1:10. Unity is what God wants for us. This is not only unity in appearance but unity in God.

- **Ephesians 2:8-10** says, "For it is by grace you have been saved, through faith — and this is not from yourselves, it is the gift of God — not by works so that no one can boast. For we are God's handiwork, created in Christ Jesus to do good works, which God prepared in advance for us to do." If we're saved by faith, then isn't it vital for us to use it in our relationships and in our teams? This verse expounds the idea that we are not saved by our works or even how we perform, but we are saved in our relationships by our faith in each other.

- **Hebrews 11:1-3** "Now faith is confidence in what we hope for and assurance about what we do not see. This is what the ancients were commended for. By faith, we understand that the universe was formed at God's command so that what is seen was not made out of what was visible." The entire foundation of faith is believing in something that you cannot see. It's not measured by action because you can't see it. Think about someone's aspirations; you need faith to unlock them.

REFLECTIONS

Team unity is strengthened when built on the foundation of shared goals of winning or faith and purpose in Christ. If everything that we want from God is accessible through faith, then let's make that the foundation for all of our relationships.

- Identify within yourself areas where you feel like your faith is strong, and ask yourself why.

- Think about your team dynamic. What would it be if you were to identify one characteristic that everybody magnifies? Evaluating the thoughts, desires, and goals of the team collectively is healthy.

- Think of ways that you can incorporate faith into your current team dynamics. Are there areas within music, visuals, or prayers that could be incorporated to assist in this matter?

ACTION POINTS

Daily Declarations: Declare over yourself 1 Corinthians 1:10. First, read the verse out loud, then pray it out loud, and then ask God to cement it in your heart and mind.

Identity Journal: write out three goals that you have for your team that connect all of them to a spiritual journey with God.

Community Engagement: Encourage a teammate today with a word of affirmation or a shared scripture.

Prayer for Faith as the Foundation of Team Unity

Lord, thank you for providing us with the means
to access you and all that we do. God, we see
the value of faith in all of our endeavors.
Teach us and guide us on ways to incorporate
and build faith into the foundations of my team.
Help us to draw on the attributes of Jesus so
our purpose is profound and clear in our actions.
Thank you God for always giving us the tools
to succeed in this life. I bless you God.
In Jesus name, amen.

DAY TWENTY-ONE

Facing Fear with Faith

“

Once you give them the power to tell you you're great, you've also given them the power to tell you you're unworthy. Once you start caring about people's opinions of you, you give up control.

”

—RONDA ROUSEY

Continuously throughout the Bible, we are reminded to go through life without fear. Jesus would always turn to his disciples and say do not be afraid. Fear is the exact opposite of faith. Fear places value on uncertainty that brings confusion and destruction. Jesus knew this about us as he reminded us to be filled with faith in moments when we would typically want to fear.

ARE YOU AFFECTED BY FEAR?

As you grow up, you may not think you're affected by fear. However, fear plays out in many ways. It demonstrates itself in trepidation and inaction. It's also visible in our indecision and confusion. There are many levels of fear, and everyone faces it practically every day in some small or big way. Rather than discount it as something that doesn't affect you, realize that if you are not walking in perfect faith, then you have some fear that you're facing. It also impacts your ability to focus on future opportunities that present themselves to you as a believer and athlete.

You're not alone in this. Everyone is fighting some level of fear in their life, and sometimes it's healthy to identify this. For, when a bear is attacking you, it's good for you to be afraid and want to run away. In the case of faith, fear and reservations in your heart and mind will only hold you back from apprehending what God has in store for you. It's better to give your fear to God and replace it with faith. This will reaffirm your decision to partner with God in this endeavor and help you prioritize your heart and mind to focus on the right things. How can you compete at the highest levels if your mind is filled with fear? It's impossible. However, what is possible is performing at the highest levels when your mind, heart, and emotions are filled with faith.

Rather than thinking about what could go wrong, let's consider what God has in store and think about all the things that could go right. Faith will give you the vision to see what's possible for yourself and for the world around you. Faith is like turning the light on in a dark room. Now you know it's possible because you have an illuminated path.

SCRIPTURES ON FACING FEAR

There are so many scriptures that remind us of stop signs and warning signs in life. One of the most predominant stop signs you will see in the Bible is "do not fear". More than a suggestion, it's a commandment for us to realize the destruction that comes with fear. We must look to God in the word, see the invitation that is inside of faith, and embrace it.

- **Isaiah 41:10:** "So do not fear, for I am with you; do not be dismayed, for I am your God. I will strengthen you and help you; I will uphold you with my righteous right hand." When God says he is with you, that is a promise that you can hold on to. Essentially, what he is saying is I completely understand what you're going through, and I will be there to support you.

- **Psalm 46:1-3:** "God is our refuge and strength, an ever-present help in trouble. Therefore we will not fear, though the earth give way and the mountains fall into the heart of the sea, though its waters roar and foam and the mountains quake with their surging."

(NIV) The enduring promise of God being our ever-present help in a time of trouble is something we should never forget. When we feel fear, we might want to isolate ourselves, but in Psalms 46, we are invited to run into God's arms because he is our refuge and strength.

- **1 John 4:18:** "There is no fear in love. But perfect love drives out fear, because fear has to do with punishment. The one who fears is not made perfect in love" (NIV). The juxtaposition of fear here is love. If you have perfect love, then you don't have fear. We have a very clear target to set our hearts and minds on to pursue perfect love to eradicate any fear in our lives.

REFLECTIONS

Fear can be a significant barrier to performance. Faith in God's presence, truth in His word, and time in prayer give us the courage to face our fears. When we look to God, we unlock our potential to do impossible things, set records, and become the best version of ourselves.

- Identify a fear you face in your sport. Pray for God's strength to overcome it.
- Contemplate on the areas where you might have fear in your heart and in your mind. You should embrace those areas and invite God in instead of ignoring them.
- Measure your performance when you have trepidation and hesitation versus your performance when you are filled with faith.

ACTION POINTS

Daily Declarations: Anytime you feel the limitations of fear, declare to yourself that God is with you and all things are possible. Consider right now the time or area where you fear and speak to yourself the word of God.

Identity Journal: Journaling your testimony is really helpful for you to see the progress in which your faith is growing and your connection with God is strengthening. Write down where you are today so you can look back in the future and see where he's brought you.

Community Engagement: Fear only brings division, so the next time you evaluate your opponent, make sure that you are optimistic about your plans. Don't give them one inch of territory that doesn't belong to them. Fill your heart with faith about who you are and what you're capable of.

Prayer for Facing Fear with Faith

Lord, thank you for giving me faith to overcome any fear that I may have. You are my refuge and my strength, and you drive out fear with your presence. Thank you, God, for giving me faith in the areas in which I feel weak and uncertain. You feel my heart and my mind, and you give me the truth and courage to push beyond the mental and emotional barriers that I perceive in my life so that I may accomplish great things.
In Jesus' name, amen.

DAY TWENTY-TWO
Gratitude in Victory and Defeat

“

Believe me, the reward is not so great without the struggle.

”

—WILMA RUDOLPH

Having gratitude goes beyond even the game. Whether you win or lose, who you are is more important. You may not feel like it in the moment because, of course, you want to win, but you have a lot of life to live, and who you become is more important. Many consider gratitude a show or performance. For example, showing someone that you're grateful is a performance that you do for them. Gratitude is far greater than any expressed action.

Gratitude is a contemplative attitude of the heart. On a spiritual side, gratitude actually gives you access to God. It may seem simple because it's a part of our culture to be thankful and have gratitude, but it actually unlocks heaven for our lives. Thankfulness is much like faith in that it's an invisible attribute that we have access to. When we demonstrate posture gratitude, we're actually opening up the opportunity for God to use us in Great and Mighty things because we have his will in our hearts.

The ultimate test for us is not just to be thankful when things are going great but also when things aren't going great. When we're losing in our game, and there's no way we could come back, try being grateful then. This is what the Bible commands of us, though, that we be thankful in all things. To be grateful for all things, we need to see the bigger picture because we often get caught up in the moment. Once we realize that our lives are filled with purpose and we have an everlasting life to live with Jesus, we will prioritize the things that he says are important, like having a grateful heart in times of goodness and in times of difficulty.

SCRIPTURES ON GRATITUDE

The word of God constantly reminds us about our inner world, our thoughts, our heart considerations, and our emotions. As we keep those in check with God's will, we will unlock ourselves to our greatest potential in life. God will be with us, and we will not be fighting against him because of our heart attitude.

- **1 Thessalonians 5:18** - "Give thanks in all circumstances; for this is God's will for you in Christ Jesus." This verse is a tremendous invitation. Give thanks in all circumstances, for this is the will of God for you! We go through a lot of ups and downs in life, and God is asking us to be thankful even when we are down because of what it does to our hearts. This is powerful.

- **Psalm 37:26** – "They [the righteous] are always generous and lend freely; their children will be a blessing." Gratitude and generosity go hand in hand in the Bible. Is there gratitude in our hearts? Are we all so generous with our time and money? This creates an inheritance for us and for our children's children.

- **Psalm 112:5** – "Good will come to those who are generous and lend freely, who conduct their affairs with justice." Our futures are set based on the attitudes that are in our heart. if we carry generosity and gratefulness then good will come to us. this is a promise from God.

REFLECTIONS

Whether in victory or defeat, gratitude keeps our hearts aligned with God's greater purpose for our lives. Of course, we strive for greatness, but we also need to see the value in our character and our response. As we keep evaluating our hearts in our minds, we will accept all that comes from God and reject what doesn't.

- Reflect on a recent victory or defeat. Offer thanks for both, seeking to learn from each experience. And take ownership of doing it openly at your next opportunity.

- Consider the commonalities that you have in your heart. How often do you consider gratitude as a primary core value of yours?

- Remember the last time you were extremely grateful for someone next to you? Why were you grateful, and how did you tell them about it?

ACTION POINTS

Daily Declarations: "I am" statements are something that God introduced in the Old Testament. In today's daily declaration, declare over yourself how thankful you are for God, your family, your opportunities, Etc. You don't need to feel thankfulness to be thankful.

Identity Journal: List out the last five times that you felt extremely grateful. Identify why and look at the context of that situation so you can repeat it.

Community Engagement: Share your thoughts with those around you. The next time you meet with your team, tell them how thankful you are for them and name an attribute or characteristic associated with it.

Prayer for Gratitude in Victory and Defeat

Lord, thank you for helping me train my heart
to be filled with gratitude and gratefulness
regardless of how I feel. I know gratitude goes
beyond our logical mind because it opens our
hearts to inconceivable things. You've shown
gratitude in the midst of the highest moments
in your life and the lowest moments.
Help me find your perspective in the midst
of my mountain top experiences and the valleys.
Thank you, God, for always being my guide.
In Jesus's name, amen.

DAY TWENTY-THREE

The Discipline of Forgiveness

"

We must develop and maintain the capacity to forgive. He who is devoid of the power to forgive is devoid of the power to love.

"

—MARTIN LUTHER KING JR.

Every day, we are challenged by people who wrong us somehow. Maybe one of your teammates took credit for something you did, or it was a family member who misused your trust which made you mad. We constantly put ourselves in situations where emotions and physical aggression can be elevated. This means we're going to be wrong, and people will hurt us. There's practically no way around it in competitive sports. This is why, in sports and in life, we need to have a very strong discipline to deploy forgiveness quickly and thoroughly. Many can probably relate to when they were younger, and their parents told them to forgive their sibling or their friend. Forgiveness is far greater than in the exchange of words. It's the ability for you to move on, and release that person or situation of the offense it caused you.

There's a great misconception about forgiveness, and it's built around this idea that you're doing some favor for the person who wronged you. Nothing could be further from the truth. The only person that is negatively affected by unforgiveness is you. See, someone could have been too aggressive or went out of their way to actually attack you, and they're perhaps happy to just move on with their life, but if you have unforgiveness towards them, then it will keep you from moving on with yours. Also, that unforgiveness will hold your inner peace hostage.

Slowly but surely, your relationships will wither and start to self-destruct if you have unforgiveness towards another person. The foundation of trust that you may have with them is now starting to erode, and bitterness will creep in. This will actually change your heart and, in turn, change your actions towards them. Having a discipline of forgiveness is not a hall pass on not having boundaries. Boundaries are very good to have, especially if someone has wronged you. However, it's up to you to forgive because your life depends on it. When you're given the option to forgive, do it quickly and deeply. It'll allow you to move on so much faster, and the people who decide to harbor unforgiveness will be held back for years.

SCRIPTURES ON FORGIVENESS

The common theme in the New Testament portion of the bible is forgiveness. We've all heard about it and generally have a sense of what it means. However, the ability to forgive someone for their wrongdoing or even sins against you is Supernatural. You're relying on the faith that God gives you and extending that to someone else. It is an incredibly powerful gift that we should not underestimate.

- **Ephesians 4:31-32** - "Get rid of all bitterness, rage and anger, brawling and slander, along with every form of malice. Be kind and compassionate to one another, forgiving each other, just as in Christ God forgave you." The standard has been set. God gave us a perfect example in Christ Jesus. The reason why he gave us this perfect example is because we can live free of unforgiveness. He knows that it will bring us health and longevity.

- **Mark 11:25**—And whenever you stand praying, forgive, if you have anything against anyone, so that your Father also who is in heaven may forgive you your trespasses." Ooh, this scripture is very compelling. The proposition here is that if we don't forgive others, then God may withhold forgiveness from us. This means we should forgive all of our trespasses deeply and quickly.

- **1 John 1:9** - "If we confess our sins, he is faithful and just to forgive us our sins and to cleanse us from all unrighteousness." The confession of sin is not just the same thing with your words. It's a confession from the heart. Do you truly mean, and are you willing to change? Forgiveness is released when we have a true confession. It's also released to us when we are not desiring for the worst to happen to the person that has offended or hurt us.

REFLECTIONS

Forgiveness can be as challenging as any physical discipline but is essential for spiritual health and team dynamics. In order to show up and be the best version of yourself you need to let go of the past and move on, even if it's challenging. The exact same scenario presents itself when we have a bad play, and we need to show up on the next play and not let the former things hold us down.

- Distinguish the difference between having boundaries and forgiveness. You can forgive someone but still have boundaries so they don't wrong you again.

- Assess within your life and your heart whether or not you are holding or harboring unforgiveness. If you are, you know what to do.

- Ask yourself, are you having a hard time forgiving yourself for something?

- Having open dialogue with people who have wronged you is really healthy, especially if you're trying to work out your forgiveness. It's better to talk openly than not say anything at all and become bitter.

ACTION POINTS

Daily Declarations: Declare daily the forgiveness that God has given you. If you're still working out forgiveness for the people around you and for yourself, then embrace the forgiveness God has for you and extend it to others.

Identity Journal: It may seem cheesy to write down people that you forgive them, but it's extremely powerful because you documented your forgiveness, and you can't go back on it now because God did the exact same thing for you.

Community Engagement: Choose to forgive someone who has wronged you, whether in or out of your sport. Consider sharing your decision with a mentor or friend for accountability. It will be the most powerful application in your journey.

Prayer for Discipline of Forgiveness

Lord, thank you for showing me what forgiveness is.
I know I'm not hurting anyone other than
myself by harboring unforgiveness.
You've released me of all my debts and my sins,
and therefore, I should find a way to release those
around me who have harmed me
and come against me.
Thank you, God, for showing me
what true forgiveness is. You are so good to me;
I want Your Love and compassion to fill my heart
so that I may be like you. Show me how to walk out
forgiveness in every moment of my day
so that I can not restrict my growth.

DAY TWENTY-FOUR
The Witness of Work Ethic

"

You are never really playing an opponent. You are playing yourself, your own highest standards, and when you reach your limits, that is real joy.

"

—ARTHUR ASHE

When you begin to serve God, everything you do is in service of him. This goes for everything you say, your character, your actions, and, of course, your work ethic. It's not just that you're representing God in some way to the people around you. This is the case because there are those around you who don't know Christ, and if you profess to know him, then you should be held to a higher standard so that they may find Christ in you.

Even more important than that is the idea that everything you put your hands into is an effort you're putting forth for God. When you desire excellence in your sport and show up on time and over-perform, you're doing it for God, God, and yourself. This isn't just a fun idea that you are trying to be the best version of yourself to impress God; it's a relational idea. It's like a kid doing their very best to impress their father. They're meticulous in their process and over-committed to doing everything they possibly can to make their dad proud. God loves this type of heart attitude because it means you're prioritizing him in your work ethic.

One of the best ways that the world measures excellence and success is in our work ethic. When people around you can see visible signs of greatness, prosperity, and health, it's attractive. That attractiveness is a way that we witness the world around us. We preach the gospel with our actions and sometimes with our words. Our goal is to become witnesses to our excellence and to outperform everyone around us so much that they desire to be us and ask us how we do it. Curiosity always opens up the door for greater things. It's an exciting day when people desire to know how you do it so well.

SCRIPTURES ON WORK ETHIC

Our work ethic is a part of our lives. It's impossible to separate ourselves from it. So if we're going to be about our work, then we might as well make it about God. This will connect the spiritual reality to our physical reality, and we will find everlasting joy in it.

- **Colossians 3:23-24** - "Whatever you do, work at it with all your heart, as working for the Lord, not for human masters, since you know that you will receive an inheritance from the Lord as a reward. It is the Lord Christ you are serving." The imagery in this verse is fascinating because we are to perceive the people who were serving in life as Christ. If we can see Jesus and the people around us, then we will remove all the barriers and excuses for loving them completely and truthfully.

- **Genesis 2:15:** "The Lord God took the man and put him in the Garden of Eden to work it and take care of it" (NIV). One of the first invitations we see in Genesis is given to Adam to go to work. Many people skip over this, but it's an invitation for all generations to work and enjoy their work. Work is not just a byproduct of sin. Work is partnership with God. That's why we see redemptive work taking place in the New Testament.

- **Ecclesiastes 9:10** "Whatever your hand finds to do, do it with all your might, for in the realm of the dead, where you are going, there is neither working nor planning nor knowledge nor wisdom." (NIV) In this verse, we see a high calling available. Whatever you do, do it with all your might. This is an internal call for us to become the best versions of ourselves and not hold back.

REFLECTIONS

Your work ethic in training and competition serves as a witness to your teammates and audience, reflecting your service to Christ and your sports career. Everything you do is being watched by your peers, your family, and the little ones. They see how you react to the small things in life and measure your posture towards work as they're developing their own. It's time to be a witness in our actions because everyone is watching.

- Think about what makes excellence in your craft and ask yourself how you can reproduce it.
- Who is someone around you who has a really good work ethic? Ask yourself why they do.
- Think of a Biblical example of someone who received a witness from God because of someone else's work ethic. it's great to find examples to accentuate the characteristics of God. Example: Paul and Timothy.

ACTION POINTS

Daily Declarations: If you feel lazy, sometimes declare the opposite in your life. If you feel like a procrastinator, speak the opposite over your life. Repeat the verse in Colossians 3:23 over your life until you feel it inside.

Identity Journal: Identify three characteristics you would consider to be strong work ethic traits. Journal those characteristics and try to identify where you are as they relate to you.

Community Engagement: Approach today's tasks, training, or competition with the mindset of serving Christ, not just achieving personal or team goals. Come with a spirit of excellence. See Daniel Chapter 6:3 NKJV

Prayer for Work Ethics

Lord, thank you for demonstrating a strong and amazing work ethic throughout the Bible. Adam, in the beginning of Genesis, was invited to work and take care of everything you gave him. This is an invitation for us to partner with you in our work. There's joy in putting our hands to work and building something beautiful. Thank you for showing us that you weren't afraid to work as a carpenter or a master builder. I love that about you. You're always out building and showing others how to build. Thank you, Jesus. In Jesus, amen.

DAY TWENTY-FIVE

The Role of Patience in Personal Growth

"

Patience and persistence are two characteristics that differentiate the professional from the amateur.

"

—CRISTIANO RONALDO

In sports, we are so outcome-focused because the pinnacle of a season is the accomplishment at the end. This is a great thing to work towards and plan for. However, in life, our greatest achievements are along the way instead of at the end. Each and every day contributes to our dreams, hopes, and desires. We don't want to discount the large majority of our lives only to measure ourselves based on one achievement at the end. Otherwise, we would be missing out on some of the most amazing experiences and processes.

It is invigorating to see the potential within yourself in a sport and life, and the desire to become the very best fills this with excitement and adrenaline. I know many experience this at a very young age because they can see someone else excelling in anything they desire.

Immediately, our hearts and minds want to become the very best now, and tension arises between who we are and what we're capable of today versus who we will be and what we're capable of tomorrow. This tension is often present throughout life and in many of our biggest accomplishments. For example, you could desire to have the very best relationships. They don't happen in one day; they happen over your lifetime.

We must be patient and content in our aggressive pursuit of greatness. Why is this? If we're not patient in our growth journey, then we will destroy ourselves and everyone on our path. The best things in life truly do take time. Of course, some are gifted with skill sets and relationships that excel them faster and further, but for the large majority of us, we need to have a patient growth process. We must be patient and not beat ourselves up because we're not seeing premium results immediately. This was too the case for Jesus. As much as we know and recognize his potential to accomplish everything before him, he still waited until 30 to go about his father's business. The reason for his perceived delay was significant, but it also showed the fortitude that he had to apply himself to the process and be patient. This example is profound for the things we desire to accomplish in our lives. Our goals and our greatest achievements might not be on a timed delay as they were for Jesus, but the greatest things in life are worth being patient for.

SCRIPTURES ON PATIENCE IN PERSONAL GROWTH

The scriptures remind us of patience because it's a grounding perspective. Often, we're in the middle of a situation or experience, and we cannot see the end or even where we're at. We don't fully perceive God's involvement or even what the next steps may be, and we're often reminded in scripture to be patient. This patience allows us to gain a perspective and not react in a way that moves us away from where God might want us.

- **James 5:7-8** - "Be patient, then, brothers and sisters, until the Lord's coming. See how the farmer waits patiently for the land to yield its valuable crop for the autumn and spring rains. You, too, be patient and stand firm because the Lord's coming is near." In James, we see the invitation to wait for God and his return. This can be interpreted as the second coming, but it's available to you now. You might be waiting for promises from God, and the invitation is for you to recognize your opportunity to be patient and not get hasty and bound out of what God has for you.

- **Romans 12:12** says, "Rejoice in hope, be patient in tribulation, be constant in prayer." Patience and prayer are a unique partnership in the Bible. When you're in the midst of tribulation, God commands you to rest and be patient. This is a tall order because when things are heating up and getting more difficult, it is really hard for our mind, our emotions, and our hearts not to overheat. God wants us to be patient in all areas of life, including competition.

- **Galatians 6:9** says, "And let us not grow weary of doing good, for in due season we will reap, if we do not give up." As we look and find our perseverance in God, we will access grace to not grow weary in our current season. If we are able to wait and be patient, we will reap in due time.

REFLECTIONS

Growth in athletics and faith often requires patience, a willingness to wait on God's timing, and cultivation of our character. It's often not fun to wait for anything because of our propensities and our culture, but we are reminded continuously within the word of God that waiting is okay and patience is a good thing. I hope you're able to find it valuable for yourself.

- Do some introspection and evaluate yourself based on how well you adapt to abrupt change, long processes, and waiting for things to play out. This will tell you a lot about yourself.

- How well would you say you utilize self-control and delayed gratification?

- What is one thing that you were patient to achieve or receive that you are really proud of? Ask yourself about the heart and mind that you experience within that waiting period.

ACTION POINTS

Daily Declarations: Utilize the gift of self-control and speak over yourself how you are made in the image of God. He is not in a hurry to do most things because he values patience. Think of all the time delays that took place in the Bible and remind yourself, in the midst of wanting to see something happen.

Identity Journal: Write down what is hard for you to wait for. Issue your journal writing today to God. Tell him what is difficult for you to process and wait for. Be as brutally honest as you can. This will allow you to speak frankly, freely, and authentically to God. Your honest dialogue with him in your journal will be really helpful for you in processing difficult things. Don't worry about offending him; he is big enough to handle your offenses. Remember, Jesus was hung up for your hang ups!

Community Engagement: Identify an area where you're impatient for growth or results. Commit it to prayer, asking for patience and trust in God's timing. Also, ask a friend of faith to pray alongside you in this area.

Prayer for Patience in Personal Growth

Lord, thank you for showing us how to be
steadfast and patient during our growth.
Sometimes, we may feel that we want to go out
and go another way, but you always show us
a more excellent way. You speak to the depths
of who we are so that we can be consistent
and firm in our faith towards you.
You help us to be unwavering in our growth
every single day. God, thank you.
You've demonstrated your will to us
so that we may establish our own in you.
Lastly, keep us from ever giving up on ourselves
and on you. Thank you, Jesus.
In Jesus name, amen.

DAY TWENTY-SIX

Endurance in Faith and Fitness

"

Faith isn't just believing;
it's about knowing that there's a reward
for those who trust in God's plan.

"

—MANNY PACQUIAO

The endurance we are invited into in our physical endeavors is no different than our spiritual walk. Just as we would push through a practice and run faster and push harder, this opportunity is available to us in God. The very idea of endurance has been around since the beginning of humanity. Just as Adam in the garden had to sweat and toil for his fruit, this perseverance should be conveyed in every area of our lives.

There's an idea presented in Hebrews that talks about how our spirit, soul, and body are interconnected. They are very much connected and overlap with one another. An example of this is how our physical bodies speak to us in the night during our dreams. If you are exhausted or injured, oftentimes, you'll have a dream that speaks to those matters. Also, our spiritual journeys and their progression can contribute to our mental health and our physical body. This evidence is not just within the belief system but manifests equally in our spiritual, soul, and body.

We will see a tremendous reward when we pursue God with fervent endurance, just as we would any championship opportunity. Pushing aside the idea and the appearance of having a religion that is primarily meritless, we should see the reward of an active relationship with God. The more we pursue him and his will in our lives and in the lives around us, the more we will experience the fullness of who he is and his kingdom. Getting to know God is one of the greatest invitations available to us, and we should deploy significant energy, time, and resources to fall in love with Jesus and do life with him. Let us consider the endurance of running a race with God and the reward set before us.

SCRIPTURES ON ENDURANCE IN FAITH AND FITNESS

- **Hebrews 10:36** - "You need to persevere so that when you have done the will of God, you will receive what he has promised." There's a connection between the promises of God and our perseverance to wait for them. This means that there's a time to delay some promises of God, and we should develop patience so that we may inherit what God has spoken over us.

- **James 1:12** "Blessed is the man who remains steadfast under trial, for when he has stood the test he will receive the crown of life, which God has promised to those who love him." In James, we see the big bold statement of don't quit. Don't give up. Even when you're under a trial, God will reward you for your perseverance.

- **Isaiah 40:31** says, "But they who wait for the Lord shall renew their strength; they shall mount up with wings like eagles; they shall run and not be weary; they shall walk and not faint." The enduring process of renewal with God starts with waiting, but in the waiting, you're actually able to receive strength to overcome. This is a submission process to God. You're not trying to accomplish it on your own; you're partnering with him in the overcoming.

REFLECTIONS

Physical and spiritual endurance is developed through consistent effort and reliance on God's strength. We also see the reward of our endurance and patience in his fulfilled promises over our lives. As we learn to persevere and push through, we will start to see that we are strengthened inside, and we can see the goal he has for us at the end—not in our own might or our own strength, but in the Lord's strength.

- Set a long-term goal for both your faith and your athletic performance. Outline the first steps you'll take toward achieving these goals.

ACTION POINTS

Daily Declarations: Declare out loud how you will wait upon the Lord to renew your strength. Speak it over yourself and declare it outloud in the mirror to yourself. , even if you don't believe it at that moment.

Identity Journal: Endurance is showing up daily and doing the work. Your action point this week is to journal every single day. Make it a priority to write down your thoughts, prayers, and heartfelt considerations before God. You got this.

Community Engagement: Combine your investment in Fitness and training with your faith in God. Find ways to incorporate your faith into your plans to develop your physical body and skills. Consider equal devotion when you make your plans this week.

Prayer for Endurance in Faith and Fitness

Lord, thank you for teaching us the reward that's before us. You know how we're made, and the pursuit of something greater is a desire that you placed in us. As we look at you, we see your enduring personality in everything that you do. You're unrelenting in your pursuit towards us and your pursuit of the goals that are before you. Help us to understand and embrace this endurance for our minds, emotions, bodies, and spirit. Thank you, God, for being such a good guide to the best things in life. We will push on to the high prize before us.
In Jesus name, amen.

DAY TWENTY-SEVEN

The Importance of Spiritual Mentors

"

Your mentors in life are important, choose them wisely.

"

—BILL WALSH

In sports, our guides to success are typically our coaches. They can see the bigger picture and speak to individual areas in which we can improve and strategize. We also have the opportunity to have coaches speak in every area of our lives. These people are called spiritual mentors. They don't have to have an official title, but they have a visible and lasting foundation that you're able to tap into. Typically, mentors are more seasoned in life, with God, and in relationships. The difference between you and them is that they've already gone through what you're experiencing or lack.

Biblically speaking, everyone who follows Jesus is able to look to him for guidance and support. Not only did they ask him questions regularly, even if they were dumb ones, but they emulated and mirrored his actions. This type of modeling is extraordinarily helpful and encouraged in the New Testament. The Apostle Paul says if you don't know what to do, then follow me and watch me.

Just as we have coaches in our sports, we need spiritual mentors in our lives. They can see things that we can't see, including our faults, weaknesses, and blind spots. They've traveled the road ahead of us, and they're able to guide us down the path of their greatest victories and keep us from stumbling the same way that they did. In some ways, the spiritual mentor is like receiving an instant upgrade. The instant upgrade is because you don't have to go through the same mistakes to achieve your desired outcome. You can use their mistakes as stepping stones in order to be victorious.

There are so many people available right now who would be your spiritual mentor, support you, pray for you, and guide you in life. We are truly without excuses when it comes to having people speak into our process and come alongside us. It's essential that we see the value in our mentors and seek them out. Our lives will be upgraded in tremendous ways if we can utilize their strengths in the areas of our greatest needs.

SCRIPTURES ON SPIRITUAL MENTORS

- **2 Timothy 2:2** - "And the things you have heard me say in the presence of many witnesses entrust to reliable people who will also be qualified to teach others." True spiritual mentors speak from a place of being qualified. They're refined in life, and they're able to give you the fruit of that refinement. They also have your best interest in mind, not their personal gain. Enjoy the reward of their process and friendship.

- **1 Peter 5:2-3** - "Be shepherds of God's flock that is under your care, watching over them...not lording it over those entrusted to you, but being examples to the flock." In 1 Peter, we see an example of a good Mentor. They're not to control you or manipulate you but rather watch over you. The idea of watching over is a shepherding and fatherly attribute you should receive in your life.

- **Proverbs 27:17** - "As iron sharpens iron, so one person sharpens another." The only way to receive refinement is for you to be tested, and it's best that you participate in that testing and invite the refinement that comes from another.

REFLECTIONS

Just as coaches play a crucial role in your athletic development, spiritual mentors guide and help your growth in faith. If you're not convinced yet that you need a spiritual mentor or to tap into the one you have more, everyone in the Bible has one, including Jesus. At a minimum, we can always look to Jesus or the Father to guide us, but it's essential that we have people here and now who are active in our lives to help spiritually guide us.

- In what ways do you feel like your ability to receive coaching has changed you?
- Who would you say is most impactful on your life and spiritual walk? It may be multiple people.
- How would you define a spiritual mentor for yourself? Where do you want to go, and who do you want to become, with their leadership?

ACTION POINTS

Daily Declarations: Proverbs 27:17 - "As iron sharpens iron, so one person sharpens another." In today's declarations, call up someone who you would perceive as your spiritual mentor and ask them for open and honest feedback in your life. Ask them to speak to the areas that you can improve on.

Identity Journal: Consider writing out ways in your journal in which you can engage spiritual mentorship and maximize the impact in your life for the people who have something to contribute.

Community Engagement: Pray for God to highlight a spiritual mentor who can guide you in your faith journey. Reach out to them and have a conversation about helping you grow. If you already have one, reach out to express your gratitude. Remember, growth comes out of authentic surrender.

Prayer for Spiritual Mentors

Lord, thank you for placing people before us that show us the way. We have you as a perfect mentor and guide, and we also have Apostle Paul, who says emulate and mirror me if you don't have anyone else to look to. God, you're so good to give us people who will help show us a better way in their actions, principles, thoughts, and considerations. Reinforce and be firm mentors in our lives so that we're not going about our lives on our own. Where there are two or three gathered, you are in the midst. Bring the right people around us to build us up in our faith and walk.
In Jesus name, amen.

DAY TWENTY-EIGHT
Competing with Compassion

"

I really think a champion is defined not by their wins, but how they recover when they fall.

"

—SERENA WILLIAMS

Competition brings out a whole host of emotions and actions in us. Just because we're in the middle of a contested battle, it doesn't mean that we need to become evil or barbaric to those who are on the opposing side. Contrary to popular belief, we can still be good people and compete at the highest level. You don't need to manifest signs of anger, frustration, resentment, or even aggression to become the best in your sport. So much of the modern-day approach to competition is self-centered. Some athletes' motive to perform is so they look a certain way rather than perform at a high level and maintaining an equal level of moral standards, character and team accountability.

You don't need to change who you are in order to compete. The example that comes to mind is when people are typically enrolled in armed services. They're told to act a certain way, say certain things, and not display characteristics that would show them as weak-minded or weak-willed individuals. There are reasons for this training, and at the end of the day, it seems to be helpful for reducing self-will and consolidating mission and mandate. However, that's not the case for everybody else in the world. You don't need to lay down your mission and mandate in order to pick up someone else's. Of course, you want to partner with your team for common goals, but you can still be yourself in any sport. Your personality and make up should be a part of a greater expression of who God is to the masses. This goes the same for being a part of a team.

The invitation here is to recognize that you can maintain high character and compassion while actively participating in any competition. God extends his compassion to you, and you freely embrace it through salvation. The greatest thing you could do with that compassion is to not only harbor it and carry it but to demonstrate it to those who are around you. This demonstration is not only just an act of kindness like picking somebody up off the ground amid competition, but it's in your heart and your will. If God sees it as valuable, then we should, too.

SCRIPTURES ON COMPASSION

Compassion is a big subject in the Bible, and in order to understand it, we need to see it played out through God's interactions with humanity and Christ's interactions with people in front of Him. Compassion is the vehicle in which we participate in order to see the fruit of God in our lives and in the lives around us. It could be said that it's impossible to see the kingdom of God without compassion..

- **Philippians 2:3-4:** "Do nothing out of selfish ambition or vain conceit. Rather, in humility, value others above yourselves, not looking to your own interests but each of you to the interests of the others." Philippians speaks to us a very clear line on acting compassionately with everything we do. Perhaps the opposite of compassion would be selfish ambition, and we are told to refrain from that.

- **Colossians 3:12:** "Therefore, as God's chosen people, holy and dearly loved, clothe yourselves with compassion, kindness, humility, gentleness and patience." Clothe yourself in compassion. This means don't go anywhere without it. This is a very profound statement in Colossians.

- **Exodus 33:19:** "And the LORD said, "I will cause all my goodness to pass in front of you, and I will proclaim my name, the LORD, in your presence. I will have mercy on whom I will have mercy, and I will have compassion on whom I will have compassion." The Lord is demonstrating his compassion towards us in this verse, and we should see the equivalent of this verse in our lives.

REFLECTIONS

Compassion and humility should mark our interactions with opponents, recognizing their dignity and worth as individuals. As we go about competing, we shouldn't devalue anyone around us but rather see the value that God has placed in them and embrace it while beating them at their game. Compassion shouldn't sacrifice excellence; the difference is whether or not you are still a good person at the end of the competition.

- Reflect on how you can show compassion and respect in your next competition, even in the heat of the moment.

- Think back on a time when you missed it and became a different person in the heat of the moment. How did you respond, and how did it make you feel afterward? Did you like yourself afterward?

- Consider someone who is really good with compassion in your life. What did they do differently?

ACTION POINTS

Daily Declarations: Declare three verses on compassion over yourself today. Be mindful of how God is compassionate to you and declare the word of God over your heart and mind. This will allow you to see yourself differently and invite God into your process.

Identity Journal: Write out areas where you can improve your compassion for yourself and your teammates first. As you're being brutally honest with yourself, consider ways in which your self-achieving is inhibiting your growth.

Community Engagement: Be the first person to pick somebody up off the ground while in competition, even if they're not on your team. Make a point to do this in your next competition, and pay attention to your heart afterward.What attitude do you feel like you display the most in life?

Prayer for Compassion

Lord, thank you for your nature not changing with each setting and season. You showed us how to be firm and compassionate at the same time. You showed us how to be unrelenting in your pursuit and unwavering in your promise yet still very loving and kind. Help us to understand the balance between having your heart and being in difficult situations like competition. We know that everything we do is for you. Help us to understand how to extend compassion as we grow in life and competition. In Jesus name, amen.

DAY TWENTY-NINE

The Impact of a Christ-like Attitude

"

Everything I have and everything I became is because of the strength of the Lord, and through him I have accomplished everything. Not because of my strength. Only by His love, his mercy, and his strength.

"

—MARIANO RIVERA

Most of the time, we go through life and we're not really cognizant of the impact that we have on others. We just put our head down and focus on what's in front of us. Perhaps we're focused on our family and our career goals. This is totally normal and very predictable. There's something, though, that we should be mindful of as we pursue our higher calling with God and achieve success in life. The thing that we should be paying attention to is how our lives impact those around us. We might not realize it, but everyone's watching how we respond to life, including our family, our teammates, and especially our kids.

Every day, you develop more of a Christ-like attitude that disseminates into your thoughts, beliefs, and actions. Literally, your attitude speaks of your future reality because of how interconnected it is with your actions. The more you become like him, the more you will be seen like him. In turn, this creates a tremendous impact on your life personally and for everyone that's around you. Because you've embraced this belief system, not only do you think differently, but the course of your life has changed. Your impact is a derivative of your attitude. It might be hard to comprehend the expansive nature of what's available, but your life's invisible realities manifest in everything you do.

As you pursue greatness and excellence in competition, hope and anticipation are the visible signs of greatness and excellence in your life. The exact same thing happens with your walk with God. The more you pursue him, the more you become like him. This ties directly into your purpose because the whole point of pursuing him now is that you could create a reality in which he is present in your life today. This reality is going to impact every single area of your life tremendously. Everywhere Jesus went, people were changed. The same could be said of you.

SCRIPTURES ON THE IMPACT OF A CHRIST-LIKE ATTITUDE

Much of the Bible is presented to govern our thoughts and character. The very reason we have so many examples in the Bible is that we need these examples to develop our own character. The greatest invitation given to us in the New Testament is that we would take this word of God and manifest it again in the flesh. That means we become the very word that we're reading, just as Jesus did.

- **Ephesians 4:2-3** - "Be completely humble and gentle; be patient, bearing with one another in love. Make every effort to keep the unity of the spirit through the bond of peace." Our character development is of the utmost importance in the Bible. We should not overlook scripture as a suggestion but rather a requirement for us to live a thriving life.

- **Colossians 3:1-2:** "Since, then, you have been raised with Christ, set your hearts on things above, where Christ is, seated at the right hand of God. Set your minds on things above, not on earthly things." This scripture reminds us of the mind of God and our access to it. We should do away with the carnal mind and embrace the mind of Christ. His mind is available within the word of God.

- **Philippians 4:8:** "Finally, brothers and sisters, whatever is true, whatever is noble, whatever is right, whatever is pure, whatever is lovely, whatever is admirable—if anything is excellent or praiseworthy—think about such things." Our thoughts create realities, and this verse is a perfect example of that. As you dwell on things in your mind, you create them in your life and impact them tremendously.

REFLECTIONS

Your attitude, especially under pressure, can be a powerful testimony to the transformative power of Christ in your life. When people see how you respond to adversities in life, they will either want to be like you and find out how you became that way or repel you because your nature is destructive.

- Self-reflection is healthy, but introspection is mostly unhealthy. One is a means to an end, and the other is just a pity party.

- Consider how your life currently impacts others around you and ask yourself if that impact looks like Jesus.

- What attitude do you feel like you display the most in life?

ACTION POINTS

Daily Declarations: Declare God's nature over yourself. Ask yourself who God is and declare the attributes, characteristics, and even names of God over yourself. You are what you behold.

Identity Journal: Write out five ways in which you feel you can improve in your demonstration of being a christian in life and in competition.

Community Engagement: Today, practice responding to stress and pressure with humility, gentleness, and patience, whether in training or in interactions with others.

Prayer for Christ-like Attitude

Lord, thank you for living life in front of us, which is the perfect example of how we should live our lives. We know our goal is to be more like you, and you've shown us the way to live. Unlock your heart and your process so we can see the mind of God. We want to be more like you, Jesus. Illuminate the image of God in our minds so we can be more Christ-like in all that we do, think, and say. You alone are the perfect one we want to be made in the image of. Thank you for helping us grow to be more like you. In Jesus' name, amen.

DAY THIRTY
Unity in Diversity

"

Teamwork is the ability to work together toward a common vision. The ability to direct individual accomplishments toward organizational objectives. It is the fuel that allows common people to attain uncommon results.

"

—ANDREW CARNEGIE

At the beginning of the Bible, we see incredible examples of unity. One example that gives a foundation for all of life is that mankind was placed inside of Adam. The Bible says that every person came from the seed of Adam. That is extremely unifying. Even though throughout the course of humanity, we've gone our own ways and developed in our own unique and geographical areas, we all come from the same seed. Our outward appearance May be different because of our exposure to different things, including sunlight and the amount of vitamin D and carotene that our body produces. A different picture is presented if we consider the people around us to be children of Adam; we all had the same father.

Moreover, even though we're more alike than we could ever imagine, we actually have spiritual and physical bonds when we come together. Just as we understand that different body parts collaborate to accomplish common goals, we, too, experience this in life. There's a reason why God recognized and acknowledged that Adam needed a helper to accomplish the things in his life. We weren't made to do this alone. We actually received strength and benefit greatly from the collaboration of others. This is why the Bible speaks about the multitude Gathering, and he presents himself there. Where there are two, there are three; there I am in the midst.

As we process life, we should consider the benefits of others around us and be open to their impact on our lives and our futures just as you would have a relationship with a spouse. They might not be like you or even think like you, but are you a better person because of them? Are you able to upgrade your life because of their presence? Perhaps if they weren't different than you, would you be where you are today? The reflection of us being open to the people around us is a very healthy process to embrace everyone in our lives as a vital part of our growth and success. Every teammate that we have can benefit our lives in some way. You may disagree with that statement, but even if they agitate you into growth, then it's a benefit. We truly are better together, and we need to have a mindset of unity when we see others. A teammate one day may become a business partner or a lifelong friend down the road!

SCRIPTURES ON UNITY IN DIVERSITY

We may see examples in scripture that speak of people whom God sets apart, but that invitation is unified in Galatians 3. We are invited into this active relationship with God and are unified under the belief in Christ. No longer is there any separation among us. We should be open to others as equally as Christ is open to accepting us.

- **1 Corinthians 12:12-13** - "Just as a body, though one, has many parts, but all its many parts form one body, so it is with Christ. For we were all baptized by one Spirit so as to form one body—whether Jews or Gentiles, slave or free—and we were all given the one Spirit to drink." As we recognize our role, we see that we actually contribute to the lives of those around us. Then, we shall see how people contribute to our life. The interconnected nature of humanity is unmistakable; we shall embrace it.

- **Galatians 3:28** – "There is neither Jew nor Gentile, neither slave nor free, nor is there male and female, for you are all one in Christ Jesus." We Are All One in Christ Jesus and that is something to meditate on. Many in life will try to tell you otherwise but we are unified in Christ and no one can take that away.

- **Colossians** 1:16-17 – "For in him all things were created: things in heaven and on earth, visible and invisible, whether thrones or powers or rulers or authorities; all things have been created through him and for him. He is before all things, and in him all things hold together." The unity that Christ displayed in creation and in his time on the Earth is unmatched. There is no other person who has demonstrated more unity in life. We should see creation as a cohesive, beautiful tapestry made by one creator and see humanity in the same way. We are better together, and our diversity is our strength.

REFLECTIONS

A team's strength lies in its diversity; each member contributes unique skills and perspectives and is united in purpose. Even those who oppose us provide us with a thorn in the flesh that accelerates our growth. Truly, everyone around us benefits us in some way.

- Reflect on ways that you are open-minded and how you could be more open-minded in your relationships.

- Consider the ways that you currently unify people around you and how you repel them.

- What characteristics do you feel you have that bring people together, and how could you use those in the future, not only in competition but outside of it?

ACTION POINTS

Daily Declarations: Meditate on Galatians 3:28. What does "we are all one in Christ Jesus" mean to you?

Identity Journal: Make a list of your strengths and weaknesses. Write out ways in which your strengths and weaknesses bring unity or disunity. Awareness is the first step to change.

Community Engagement: Celebrate the diversity within your team. Consider how each member's unique contributions make the team stronger. Acknowledge them publicly in front of others.

Prayer for Unity in Diversity

Lord, thank you for demonstrating your nature
within creation. You show tremendous creativity
and diversity in every animal, insect, reptile,
and bird. I know that your personality
and your desire are for immense diversity.
Help us to see that in each other.
Search my heart of God and help me uncap
your priorities. Help me to see the world
the way that you see it. Many people around me
want to divide us; show me ways to unite us
just as you would. Thank you, Jesus.
I bless you. In Jesus name, amen.

Conclusion

Congratulations on completing your journey through "Know Your Playbook!" Over the past 30 days, you've delved into the depths of faith, exploring the sacred truths that guide us through life's playbook. As you conclude this devotional, remember that the end of one journey is preparing you for another.

Throughout this devotional, you've gained insights, found inspiration, and deepened your connection with the divine playbook of life. Now, as you step forward, let these truths not remain mere words on a page but become living, breathing principles guiding your every step and your growth as an athlete and believer in Jesus.

Every lesson, every reflection, and every moment spent in devotion has equipped you with the wisdom and strength to navigate life's twists and turns with faith as your compass. As you move forward, may you carry this playbook in your heart, letting it shape your decisions, guide your actions, and inspire your aspirations.

Remember, the true measure of your journey lies not in how well you understand the playbook but in how faithfully you live it out each day in every area of your lives. Let love be your playbook's language, kindness's strategy, and compassion's goal.

As you embark on the next chapter of your journey, know that you do not walk alone. The divine author of life walks beside you, ready to guide, strengthen, and empower you every step of the way. He is God, and he loves you!

So, my friends, go forth with courage, conviction, and unwavering faith. The world awaits your unique expression of God to humanity!

With heartfelt congratulations and boundless blessings.

In Jesus' name, give em heaven!!!

—Greg Hendricks

FOLLOW
GREG HENDRICKS
@greghendrickslife
@greghendrickslife
greghendricks.life
connect@greghendricks.life

Printed in the USA
CPSIA information can be obtained
at www.ICGtesting.com
CBHW061248040624
9483CB00004B/21